A HISTORY OF
the Bahá'í Faith
IN SOUTH CAROLINA

June 2022

A History of
the Bahá'í Faith
in South Carolina

For John and Barbara —
with so much love
and gratitude.

Louis Venters

Louis

THE
History
PRESS

Published by The History Press
Charleston, SC
www.historypress.com

Opposite: The Bahá'í Faith in South Carolina and the built environment, 2019. A number of sites, historic and contemporary, hold significance for the Bahá'í community. *Gregory G. Fry.*

First published 2019

Manufactured in the United States

ISBN 9781467117494

Library of Congress Control Number: 2018960979

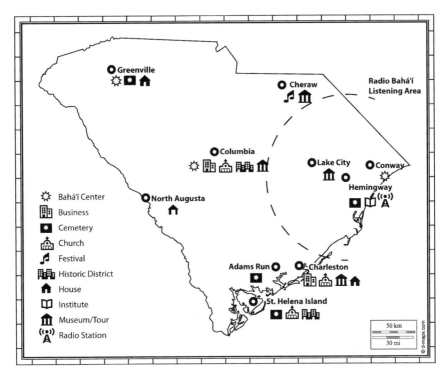

Adams Run
• Baháʼí Cemetery

Charleston
* All of the following properties are part
  of the Charleston Historic District,
  National Register of Historic Places
  (NR); the Avery Center and Old Bethel
  Church are also listed individually in
  the National Register.
• Alonzo Twine House—*private residence*
• Avery Center for African American History
  & Culture—*College of Charleston*
• Louis G. Gregory Baháʼí Museum
• Old Bethel United Methodist Church
• Westendorff Building—*private business*

Cheraw
• Dizzy Gillespie self-guided walking
  tour—*statue on Town Green, Dizzy Gillespie
  Homesite Park, other sites*
• South Carolina Jazz Festival—*third
  weekend in October, commemorating Dizzy
  Gillespie's birthday*

Columbia
• Baháʼí Center
• Parker Annex Building—*private business,
  part of Bull Street project*
• Sidney Park C.M.E. Church (NR)

• State House & African American
  Monument (NR)
• Waverly Historic District (NR)

Conway
• Baháʼí Center

Greenville
• Abercrombie House—*private residence*
• Baháʼí Center
• Baháʼí Cemetery property—*unimproved*

Hemingway
• Louis G. Gregory Baháʼí Institute
• Radio Baháʼí
• Baháʼí Cemetery

Lake City
• Ronald E. McNair Life History Center &
  Memorial Park—*museum, statue and
  gravesite*

North Augusta
• Rosemary Inn (former James U. Jackson
  residence) (NR)

St. Helena Island
• Baháʼí Cemetery
• Brick Baptist Church & Penn
  Center—*Penn Center National Landmark
  Historic District & Reconstruction Era
  National Monument*

In memory of my grandmother Rebecca Glymph Venters (1916–2009),
proud South Carolinian

Contents

June 1865

In the middle of June 1865, life was nowhere near normal in South Carolina's war-battered capital of Columbia. The slaveholders' rebellion that had begun in Charleston more than four years before had come to a disastrous end, and much of the state, which had escaped the worst of the fighting for most of the war, was a shambles. In February, a substantial portion of Columbia had burned as a phalanx of United States troops moved through the area—likely the result of burning cotton bales set on fire by fleeing Confederates and made worse by high winds and free-flowing alcohol. The mayor and city council were overwhelmed by the crisis, with many residents homeless, destitute, and hungry—and the sickly cattle that Sherman's troops had left on the green of South Carolina College were little help. In the city and surrounding countryside, the system of slavery was falling apart. While whites struggled to maintain a semblance of control, blacks were everywhere pressing their claims for freedom, social and economic justice, and membership in the body politic. Despite the chaos, schools and businesses were beginning to reopen. A U.S. Army garrison had arrived in May to set up military government, and soon the pages of the *Daily Phoenix*, a new paper that veteran journalist and Confederate loyalist Julian A. Selby had started in March, were full of orders from headquarters about the protection of freedpeople, the supervision of labor contracts, and the suppression of crime. Everyone could see that South Carolina society had been turned upside down, but there was little agreement about what kind of world should take the place of the one that was crumbling.[1]

Amid the welter of expectation, confusion, and suffering, an item from half a world away on the front page of the June 16 edition of the *Daily Phoenix* seemed perhaps incongruous. Taking up almost two full columns of the paper's five, the article was a reprint, undated and unsigned, of an 1851 letter from a medical missionary in Iran to the American Oriental Society in Massachusetts. Under the title "Bab—A Curious History," it purported to tell the story of an interesting religious figure who had appeared among the Shia Muslims of southern Iran. To later generations familiar with the ministry of the Báb, many of the salient elements are there in some form: the stainless character; the startling claim of divine authority; the revelation of holy verses with a beauty and rapidity that astonished witnesses and aroused the ire of the Shia clergy; the epistles sent to followers in all parts of the country; the devotion shown by a provincial governor; the fateful opposition of the shah; the imprisonment, torture, and ultimate execution of the Báb himself; and the bloody persecution of his followers. Yet there is no indication of the content or substance of the teachings that had so stirred a far-off land, no mention of the Báb's call for spiritual renewal and a revolution in values, his care for the status of women and the poor, his insistence that humanity stood at the threshold of a new era, or his urgent call to his followers to seek out a new and even greater Messenger of God, whose advent he said was imminent. Instead, there is a great deal of the Orientalist gaze of the American Protestant intellectual: the story is labeled a "curiosity," the Báb an "Eastern pretender," his writings "unintelligible," and his movement safely "extinguished."[2]

For most readers of the *Daily Phoenix* with more immediate concerns on their minds, the strange article probably elicited little attention. Perhaps James Woodrow, the prominent Columbia Theological Seminary professor and uncle of future U.S. president Thomas Woodrow Wilson, noticed it two columns across from his own announcement that he would resume taking students for private lessons. Either way, there is no reason to believe that the earliest known story related to the Bahá'í Faith to appear in South Carolina's press—indeed, one of the earliest in the United States as a whole—caused the slightest stir in Columbia. Like so many Romans eighteen centuries before, South Carolinians remained largely unaware of the stirrings of a new religious movement out on the tattered fringes of the "civilized" world. Little did they know that the newborn faith would not only survive brutal persecution but also grow to have a bearing on the lives of many of their descendants, that it would claim to be the source and leading edge of the zeitgeist—as one native son would put it, the "Most Great Reconstruction"—and address itself explicitly to the most challenging problems of their society, and that thousands of South Carolinians from all walks of life would come to engage its ideas, derive inspiration from its teachings, be sustained by its scriptures, and contribute to the development of its distinctive institutions and community practices.[3]

ACKNOWLEDGEMENTS

The research and writing of this book, especially since it came unexpectedly in the midst of other pressing personal and professional commitments, has left me pleasantly indebted to a number of individuals and institutions.

My heartfelt thanks to Chad Rhoad, my editor at The History Press, who had the foresight to commission this work and the patience to see it through despite numerous delays, the rest of the staff of The History Press, and to all those who reviewed all or portions of the text. Special gratitude to Roger Dahl, Rick Doering, and Edward Sevcik at the Bahá'í National Center and to the rest of the small army of archivists, too numerous to name here, who assisted in various ways with the location and acquisition of the images used in the book, and to the individuals who generously shared from their private collections, including via the South Carolina Bahá'í History Project group on Facebook.

Thanks, as ever, to the administrators, faculty, staff, and students of Francis Marion University, who make our institution such a rich working and learning environment. My special gratitude to my friends and colleagues in the History Department; to the Professional Development Committee, which funded travel to conferences where many of the ideas in this book were tested and a summer stipend to complete the preparation of the manuscript; and to Greg Fry of the Fine Arts Department, who generously contributed his time and expertise to the creation of the beautiful maps.

Special thanks as well to several friends and colleagues who have provided invaluable encouragement during the production of this book, among them Farzam and Sona Arbab, Filip Boicu, Ken Bowers, Windi Burgess, Elizabeth Ellis, Guy Mount, Annette Reynolds, Martha Schweitz, and Rob Stockman. The late Howard C. "Kip" Carter (1941–2018), the first general manager of Radio Bahá'í WLGI, was an indefatigable supporter and a storehouse of knowledge and experience.

Last but certainly not least, my eternal gratitude to the Bahá'ís of Florence, our other dear friends in the area, and my family. Special thanks to my in-laws, Barry and Marilyn Smith, and to Colleen McCullough, without whose inestimable services this book would have proven impossible to complete. Among my invaluable close friends, Greg Schweitz deserves special mention for his thoughtful reflections on my work and his consistent ability to lift my spirits. My brilliant wife, Melissa Smith-Venters, has been as committed to this project as I, and her practical, moral, and intellectual support at every step has been indispensable. Among my great pleasures in writing has been that her contributions to the South Carolina Bahá'í community toward the end of the period under consideration could be recounted here for the first time. Our extraordinary little boys, Isaiah and Micah, have grown so much as this book took shape; I eagerly look forward to the chapters that they and the other young people of South Carolina will add in the years to come.

INTRODUCTION

I n the early twenty-first century, the Bahá'í Faith is increasingly recognized as part of the social and religious fabric of South Carolina. In academia and the media, it is frequently referred to as South Carolina's second-largest religion after Christianity—the only state in the country where the Bahá'í community has grown so large. In some sense, this is a dubious distinction: in a place as overwhelmingly Protestant as South Carolina, the Bahá'ís still account for only a tiny sliver of the population. Nevertheless, the religion is disproportionately well known. A relatively large number of local Bahá'í communities, a few of which own modest properties, conduct a variety of devotional, educational, and service activities throughout the state, and over the years, they have earned a solid reputation among leaders of thought for their work in such areas as race relations, interfaith dialogue, and the moral development of children and youth. The Louis G. Gregory Bahá'í Institute in rural Georgetown County, founded in 1972 and named for the native son who first brought the faith to South Carolina, is a focal point of Bahá'í education and identity in the state and region, and a community-service radio station, broadcasting from the campus of the Institute since 1984, has brought awareness of the faith and its teachings to a substantial portion of the population in the eastern part of the state—including considerable numbers of residents and tourists in the Grand Strand. Other South Carolinians know of the Bahá'í Faith because of its association with several prominent individuals, including civil rights activist Muhiyidin Moyé (1985–2018) of

Charleston; award-winning journalist and humanitarian Susan Audé (b. 1952) of Columbia; physicist and *Challenger* astronaut Dr. Ronald McNair (1950–1986) of Lake City; and world-renowned jazz trumpeter and band leader John Birks "Dizzy" Gillespie (1917–1993) of Cheraw. Since 2003, in the heart of downtown Charleston, the community has operated the childhood home of Louis Gregory as a museum—the first Bahá'í museum in the world, and in a virtual museum-city the first dedicated to the life of a single individual.[4]

Yet in South Carolina and around the country, the remarkable story of how an obscure, "foreign," and thoroughly unorthodox new religion that placed a premium on interracial community successfully established itself in a small, poor, southern state remains underappreciated. Thankfully, however, at least that story has begun to be told. My first book, *No Jim Crow Church: The Origins of South Carolina's Bahá'í Community*, published in 2015, reconstructs the earliest history of the Bahá'í Faith in the state up to the late 1960s, and it has been well received both among historians of race and religion and among the general public. A sequel, which will bring the story up to the early twenty-first century, is currently in the research phase. This book, which I started working on as *No Jim Crow Church* went to press, is a brief companion to the other two, told substantially through a rich collection of historical photos and other images. It provides for the first time an overview of the history, practices, and culture of the Bahá'í Faith in South Carolina in its first century, beginning with the visit of the state's earliest Bahá'í teacher in 1910. For those who have read *No Jim Crow Church*, which recounts the struggles of early South Carolina Bahá'ís to build an interracial movement in the midst of the state's pervasive segregation, discrimination, and violence, the first few chapters will include much that is familiar, but the latter ones, covering the period from the late 1960s to approximately 2010, represent entirely new research. This portion of the book is the first substantial treatment anywhere of what one scholar of religion has aptly dubbed the "Carolinian Pentecost"—the series of growth campaigns in the 1970s and 1980s during which some twenty thousand people, mostly African Americans in rural areas, embraced the faith—and the unprecedented opportunities and challenges it represented for the Bahá'í community, both in South Carolina and in the country as a whole. I hope that it will contribute to a better understanding of this seminal moment—a quieter revolution than the one waged by civil rights activists, to be sure, but one that is significant in its own right—among historians and the general public as well as among American Bahá'ís themselves.[5]

This book does not attempt to provide a comprehensive introduction to the Bahá'í Faith; a number of excellent books and websites are available for that purpose. However, as the establishment and growth of the religion in South Carolina has been intimately connected with events elsewhere, readers who are new to exploring it will get a sense of its teachings and its global history and scope from the story that unfolds here. Suffice it to say that at the heart of the Bahá'í community, in South Carolina and around the world, are the lives and ministries of Bahá'u'lláh ("the Glory of God," 1817–1892), the religion's founder, and the Báb ("the Gate," 1819–1850), his prophetic herald, and the revolutionary principle of the oneness of humanity that forms the central theme of the faith's scriptures and the foundation of its organized life. Born Shia Muslims in Iran, the Báb and Bahá'u'lláh claimed that their successive revelations constituted a fresh outpouring of the divine will for humanity and the fulfillment of the prophecies of all the great religions of the past. The whole human race, they said, was infused with a new life, and the application of their teachings would, over the course of the coming centuries, weld all the peoples of the world into an organic, interdependent global commonwealth, the culmination of human evolution on this planet. In the religious language familiar to most South Carolinians, the spirit of Christ had returned "in the glory of the Father," and the day of "one fold, and one shepherd," the Kingdom of God on earth, had arrived. This startlingly original vision of radical, peaceful, global transformation was perhaps best summarized in Bahá'u'lláh's famous formulation: "The earth is but one country, and mankind its citizens."[6]

From the outset, Bahá'ís took the oneness of humanity not simply as an ideal but as the bedrock of a new identity and as a mandate for individual and collective action. Adopting the "world-embracing" vision to which their faith called them, they set out to carry its message beyond the borders of Iran and to enroll an ever-widening diversity of people as believers. By the time of Bahá'u'lláh's passing in Ottoman Palestine in 1892, the culmination of forty years of exile and imprisonment, the religion had spread to Egypt and Sudan in the west and Burma and China in the east. During the ministry of 'Abdu'l-Bahá ("Servant of Glory," 1844–1921), the Center of the Covenant, Bahá'u'lláh's eldest son and successor as head of the Bahá'í community, the faith was established in the United States, and American Bahá'ís quickly took the lead in establishing the lay governing councils that Bahá'u'lláh had called for (indeed, he forbade any form of priesthood or clergy) and in planting new outposts of the religion abroad. Both processes gained momentum under the direction of Shoghi Effendi (1897–1957), the Guardian of the Cause of God, 'Abdu'l-Bahá's eldest grandson and successor, culminating in 1963 with the election of the Universal House of Justice, the supreme governing body of the faith. During the course of the twentieth century and into the twenty-first, South Carolinians from all walks of life joined men and women from virtually every conceivable background around the world to help build the faith's highly democratic and egalitarian system of governance and distinctive collective life, enabling them to engage increasing numbers of their neighbors in the collective work of humanity's social, economic, and intellectual development.[7]

1

"TELL THEM OF REAL FREEDOM"

ORIGINS, 1910–1921

When Louis Gregory, a son of former slaves from South Carolina, first heard of the Bahá'í Faith in 1907, the new religion had been present in North America for little more than a decade. Gregory, an attorney and federal civil servant in Washington, D.C., was the first member of the African American elite—what the Atlanta University sociologist W.E.B. Du Bois termed the "Talented Tenth"—to investigate the faith's astonishing claims in earnest. In rather short order, as Gregory moved from skeptic to seeker to committed adherent, he brought his considerable gifts to bear on what became his life's mission: to assure that a nascent Bahá'í community in the United States took shape, true to the faith's central principle of the oneness of humanity, as a movement firmly committed to interracial unity; to bring the Bahá'í teachings to the attention of as many people, black and white, as would listen; and to build the capacity of the Bahá'í community to engage with the pressing issues of the day and contribute to social progress. Understandably, a great deal of his attention was directed toward the South, where 90 percent of the country's black population lived, and as a writer, administrator, and traveling teacher, he worked assiduously to turn the gaze of his fellow believers in the same direction. He was hardly alone. In his home state of South Carolina, a lone Bahá'í settler, a single woman recently emigrated from Germany, reached out to her white and black neighbors and began to discover just how difficult it would be to establish a new, interracial religious community in the heartland of America's Jim Crow order. And for one new believer in Charleston, the consequences of challenging the racial and religious status quo proved particularly perilous.

Louis Gregory, Bahá'í Leader

Born in 1874 in Charleston, South Carolina, Louis George Gregory was part of the first generation of black southerners born after the Civil War. The second son of former slaves who fled the violence of Reconstruction in rural Darlington District, he benefited from the social and economic advantages of growing up in South Carolina's largest city, including access to the state's first system of free public education. While adversity continued to stalk his family—in the city's overcrowded conditions, his father, brother, and mother all died of communicable diseases before he finished high school—he relied on his maternal grandmother and his stepfather, a skilled carpenter, for emotional and practical support. He graduated from the missionary-run Avery Normal Institute, the city's only black school with a college-preparatory program, and with his stepfather's help went on to study at Fisk University in Nashville, one of the best institutions of higher learning for blacks in the country. After a short stint back in Charleston teaching at Avery Institute and

Louis George Gregory (1874–1951), probably on his graduation from Fisk University, 1896. One of the most accomplished teachers and administrators in the early American Bahá'í movement, Gregory introduced the faith to much of the Deep South, including his native South Carolina. *National Bahá'í Archives.*

editing a weekly newspaper, Louis Gregory entered the law school at Howard University in Washington, D.C. When he graduated in 1902, he was among only a few hundred black lawyers in the country.[8]

It was hardly a surprise that Louis Gregory chose to stay in Washington, first in private practice with another Howard graduate and then taking a job as a legal clerk at the U.S. Department of the Treasury. In South Carolina and across the South, the relative optimism of Reconstruction had given way to a social and political situation that was increasingly untenable for African Americans, and in the decades before the Great Migration brought legions of black southerners into northern industrial centers, the federal capital was a refuge. Believing that his education and position brought with them social responsibility, Louis Gregory became active in the local Republican Party, went to court on behalf of victims of discrimination, spoke out in the press against segregation and lynching and, in at least one case, staged a sit-in demonstration at a segregated lunchroom in Washington's city hall. He served as president of the Bethel Literary and Historical Society, one of the community's oldest and most prestigious cultural organizations, and the local African American newspaper lauded him as "one of the most gifted writers and speakers in this country." In 1905, when Du Bois and other race leaders formed the Niagara Movement to press for full civil and political rights for African Americans, Gregory eagerly took up the cause.[9]

So, in 1907, when a friend and officemate at the U.S. Treasury, an elderly white man from Maryland, told Louis Gregory he should go investigate a strange-sounding new religion, he initially brushed it off. Gregory later recalled that after "seeking, but not finding Truth," he had "given up" on the Congregationalism of his youth—indeed, on any and all religion—as a means for solving the pressing issues of the day. He finally agreed to attend a Bahá'í meeting only out of courtesy. Despite his misgivings, the experience astonished him. The meeting's host, a southern white woman, welcomed him with disarming warmth, and the speaker gave a "brief but vivid" account of the "appearances of the Bab and Baha'u'llah and of the great persecutions and martyrdoms in Persia." He investigated the faith for more than a year, attending meetings in the homes of the southern white woman and her husband, Pauline and Joseph Hannen, and of new black converts. Sometimes, he brought friends. Gradually, he later recalled, his "mental veils were cleared away, and the light of assurance mercifully appeared within." In the teachings of the new faith, Gregory found his social and political concerns broadened and refined and, quite to his surprise, harmonized with the deepest longings of his ancestral Christianity—the prophetic promise of a reign of justice and righteousness on earth that had so shaped black South Carolinians' understanding of the Civil War and Reconstruction. Moreover, his encounter with the Bahá'í Faith inspired a rekindling of personal religious feeling, as the Hannens taught him "how to pray." In the summer of 1909, he became, in his words, a "confirmed believer," wrote a personal confession of faith, and sent it to 'Abdu'l-Bahá, the living head of the religion, still a prisoner of conscience in Palestine.[10]

The latter's reply to Gregory's declaration of faith arrived in November 1909, and it set the course of his service to the faith for the rest of his life. 'Abdu'l-Bahá wrote:

I hope that thou mayest become...the means whereby the white and colored people shall close their eyes to racial differences and behold the reality of humanity, that is the universal unity which is the oneness of the kingdom of the human race....Rely as much as thou canst on the True One, and be thou resigned to the Will of God, so that like unto a candle thou mayest be enkindled in the world of humanity and like unto a star thou mayest shine and gleam from the Horizon of Reality and become the cause of the guidance of both races.

'Abdu'l-Bahá (1844–1921), Bahá'u'lláh's son and successor as worldwide head of the Bahá'í community, 1912. After 'Abdu'l-Bahá spoke at the NAACP's fourth annual convention during his visit to North America, W.E.B. Du Bois featured him prominently in the organization's national journal. *From the* Crisis.

For Gregory, the letter (called a "tablet" from the Arabic *lawh*) was a mandate to pursue the work of interracial unity and social justice along a number of lines: bringing the message of the faith to larger numbers of African Americans and to progressive whites; working with like-minded groups and individuals to promote interracial cooperation and fellowship and create alternatives to Jim Crow; and building the Bahá'í movement's fledgling administrative bodies as laboratories of interracial democracy—all of which received a significant boost in 1912 when 'Abdu'l-Bahá, freed by the Young Turk revolution, toured North America for almost a year to propagate his father's teachings. Over the next four decades, as a prolific writer for Bahá'í publications, one of the community's most active traveling teachers, and a member of the faith's elected national body for a total of sixteen years between 1912 and 1946, Louis Gregory kept race and social justice at the forefront of the emerging American Bahá'í movement. His work set the tone and laid the foundations for the development of the faith in South Carolina and across the South.[11]

Charleston

In the fall of 1910, heartened by the emerging interracialism of the local Bahá'í community in Washington—the first city where the faith had been established that had a substantial black population—and determined to introduce the faith to more African Americans, Louis Gregory set out by train on a speaking tour of Virginia, North Carolina, South Carolina, and Georgia, which together accounted for about one-third of the country's black population. While not the first Bahá'í to travel or reside in the South, Gregory was certainly the first who was both a black professional and a native of the region, a combination that assured him ready audiences among African Americans and opportunities to contact open-minded whites. He spoke to hundreds of people in churches, schools, social organizations, and private homes in eight cities and towns, including Richmond, Virginia; Enfield, Durham, and Wilmington, North Carolina; Charleston, South Carolina; and Macon, Georgia. He probably also visited Augusta, Georgia, and either Aiken or North Augusta, neighboring towns in South Carolina. The trip was a significant advance in a process by which the country's black population would encounter the Bahá'í Faith and its teachings. While there were a handful of believers in Virginia, it was likely the first foray by a Bahá'í into the Carolinas and Georgia.[12]

After his stay in Wilmington, Louis Gregory traveled to Charleston via Florence, a railroad junction less than ten miles from the plantation where his mother and grandmother had been enslaved. At home in Charleston, he found plenty of friends, associates, and family members who were receptive to the message he had come to share. "Am just having the time of my life!" he wrote to Joseph Hannen. He had "numerous engagements to speak in churches, halls, and…parties" and to the Colored Ministerial Union. He had already met with an Episcopal priest, who, it turned out, already knew something of the Bahá'í Faith from a visit to Green Acre, a Bahá'í-owned summer colony on the southern coast of Maine. On November 8, 1910, Gregory was the featured speaker at a "Lecture and Musicale" at the Carpenters' Hall, a meeting that was probably arranged by his stepfather. None of the ministers on the program showed up, so Gregory "had the attentive audience to face alone, yet not alone, for the Spirit was powerful." Altogether, he told Hannen, "the whole city seems interested."[13]

Gregory also met with some or all of Charleston's six black attorneys, most of whom he probably already knew. He wrote to Hannen that the lawyers "seem[ed] favorable" to the Bahá'í teachings, and one of them, Alonzo Edgar

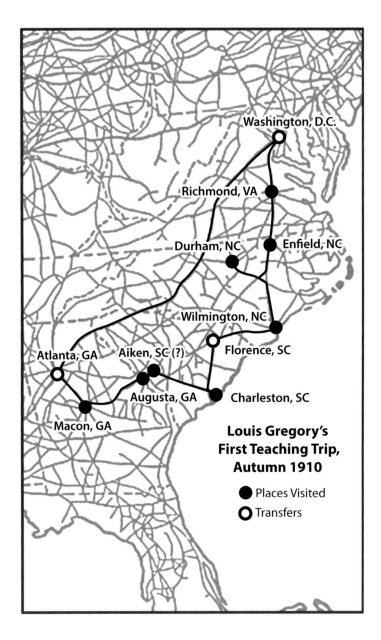

**Louis Gregory's
First Teaching Trip,
Autumn 1910**

● Places Visited
○ Transfers

Approximate route of Louis Gregory's first Bahá'í teaching trip, autumn 1910. Taking advantage of his personal and professional connections, Gregory shared the faith directly with some nine hundred people, black and white, noting that "people were found who accepted the great Message" in every town he visited. *Gregory G. Fry.*

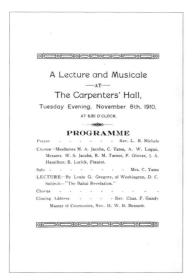

A Lecture and Musicale
—AT—
The Carpenters' Hall,
Tuesday Evening, November 8th, 1910,
AT 8.30 O'CLOCK.

PROGRAMME

Prayer . . . . . . Rev. L. R. Nichols
Chorus—Mesdames M. A. Jacobs, C. Yates, A. W. Logan,
Messers. W. S. Jacobs, R. M. Turner, F. Glover, J. A.
Hamilton; E. Lorick, Pianist.
Solo . . . . Mrs. C. Yates
LECTURE—By Louis G. Gregory, of Washington, D.C.
Subject---"The Bahai Revelation."
Chorus
Closing Address . . . . Rev. Chas. F. Gandy
Master of Ceremonies, Rev. H. W. B. Bennett.

Program, "A Lecture and Musicale at the Carpenters' Hall," Charleston, November 8, 1910. Louis Gregory's stepfather was probably a member of the carpenters' union and helped arrange the event. *National Baháʾí Archives.*

Twine, had identified himself as a believer. Twine accompanied Gregory to his other engagements in Charleston and arranged at least one more, a talk to the Young People's Union at New Tabernacle Fourth Baptist Church. After his successful stay in Charleston, Louis Gregory traveled on to Augusta and Macon, and Alonzo Twine remained, the only Baháʾí in his city. About the same age as Gregory, Twine was a graduate of Claflin University in Orangeburg, South Carolina, a trustee of Old Bethel Methodist Church, and an active participant in black Charleston's political and cultural life. Gregory likely left him with some Baháʾí books, and on at least one subsequent occasion, a Sunday evening gathering at his own church, Twine gave a public address about the religion he had espoused. Apparently, however, his efforts to teach the faith made him some enemies. In October 1911, almost exactly a year after Louis Gregory's visit, Twine was arrested on the streets of Charleston, judged insane, and committed to the state mental hospital in Columbia. The *Washington Bee*, one of the most influential African American newspapers in the country, ran the story under the provocative headline, "He Had Wrong Religion." According to the article, the cause of Twine's illness was his having forsaken "the faith of his fathers" and accepting the "new and...strange kind of religion" called the "religion of Bahai." A Savannah paper carried a similar story, lamenting the "brilliant and promising young attorney" who had lost his mind when he "severed his connection" with his church and embraced a new religion introduced to Charleston by "Louis Gregory of Washington, D.C."[14]

It is unclear exactly what circumstances led to Twine's confinement or if he was even sick at all. It is entirely plausible that opposition and ostracism in the wake of his conversion contributed to a mental breakdown. On the other hand, Twine lived in the heart of a society with a long record of labeling troublesome blacks as insane. Whether or not Twine was actually mentally ill, the pastor of his church, members of his family, local police, physicians, and

11. How many attacks of mental disease has the patient had? Give date and duration of each attack.
Answer. *One . 29th. Sept 1911 to date*

12. Did the attack or attacks come on suddenly, or slowly and gradually?
Answer. *Suddenly*

13. Give some prominent symptoms of each attack?
Answer.

14. If...*she*...has been in any asylum or hospital for the insane, state in what asylum? How often and how long?
Answer. *No*

15. What is the supposed cause of the present attack?
Answer. *religion*

16. Has...*she*...ever been overworked mentally or physically, overtaxed or strained in mind or body?
Answer. *No*

17. Has...*she*...loss of property, or sickness, or death of relatives, or any ill treatment or privation, caused unusual anxiety or trouble?
Answer. *No*

18. How long since the indications of the present attack of insanity appeared? What were the first evidences?
Answer. *abt. 6 mos.. Religion obsession*

19. Is the derangement on various subjects or on a single one? On what subject or subjects is...*she*...deranged? *religion*
Answer. *one*

20. In what way is the disease now exhibited?
Answer. *Religious excitement*

21. Is...*she*...regular in work, or lazy or incapable of labor?
Answer. *regular*

22. Has...*she*...any delusions? If so, what are they?
Answer. *Religious*

23. Is...*she*...destructive of clothing or property?
Answer. *No*

24. Is...*she*...irritable, quarrelsome, noisy, filthy or indecent?
Answer. *Noisy*

Commitment papers for Alonzo Twine, 1911 (detail). Less than a year after becoming a Bahá'í, Twine was sent to the pestilential state insane asylum for "religious [obsession]." No photograph of Twine has survived. *South Carolina Department of Archives and History.*

a judge all appear to have played a role in his institutionalization. According to legal testimony by his mother, there had been "indications of [the] present attack of insanity" for some six months prior in the form of "religious [obsession]," he was suffering religious "delusions," and he was "deranged" on the subject of religion. When asked if he had remained regular in his work or been destructive, irritable, or quarrelsome, she testified only that he had been "noisy." Apparently, this sounded dangerous enough to a probate judge, who signed a commitment order and had Twine admitted to the South Carolina State Hospital for the Insane. Shortly after his arrival, he was diagnosed with manic-depressive disorder, but like most black patients in the facility, he apparently received little or no treatment.[15]

Even if Twine was of perfectly sound mind when he entered the State Hospital, a short time there certainly would have been enough to undo him. A legislative investigation in 1909 had revealed the place to be a nightmarish pesthole, particularly for black inmates. In the Parker Building and a newly-built annex meant to relieve severe overcrowding, black male patients slept on vermin-infested straw on the floor of their cells, often dressed in little more than rags. More than a quarter of Parker's residents died each year, mostly from tuberculosis, which was easily transmitted in the crowded and filthy conditions, and pellagra, a debilitating niacin deficiency caused by the meager diet of grits, cornbread, fatback, and coffee. Even white patients complained that they seldom saw doctors; for black patients, surviving records give no indication of any psychological or medical treatment beyond perfunctory examinations upon arrival. While black patients were judged unfit for free society, they were apparently competent enough to build new hospital buildings, maintain the extensive grounds, milk the cows, and do the laundry—all at significant cost savings to South Carolina's taxpayers.[16]

To add insult to injury, Twine's former pastor from Charleston, Reverend I.E. Lowery, took away what was likely his last remaining solace: a single Bahá'í book. In comments published more than a decade later, Lowery wrote that when he was transferred to a church in Columbia, Twine's parents had asked him to visit Twine in the State Hospital. "The first time we called to see him," Lowery recalled, "he held in his hand a little pamphlet, and we asked him for it. He readily gave it to us, and we found it to be a book on the Bahai religion. We took it from him and brought it home, knowing that it was this that caused him to lose his mind." Alonzo Twine survived three years in the abominable conditions of the asylum before succumbing to pellagra. He died on October 26, 1914, probably alone and completely demented in the

Parker Building, South Carolina State Hospital for the Insane, circa 1905. Along with the Parker Annex, it housed black male patients when Alonzo Twine died of pellagra in 1914. It was demolished in the 1980s, but the Parker Annex still stands. *Richland Library, Columbia, South Carolina.*

last stages of the disease. At Twine's parents' request, Lowery brought the broken body back to Charleston for a funeral at Old Bethel.[17]

While no surviving records indicate Louis Gregory's response to Alonzo Twine's fate, it was a sadly familiar situation. Even in the relative openness of Washington, in an era when respectability politics held powerful sway among aspiring African Americans, friends thought Louis Gregory had become "mentally unbalanced" when he had become a Bahá'í. A prominent mentor at Howard, among others, thought he was "blasting all hopes of a career," and a vicious newspaper columnist implied that he was risking his soul, his mind, and his manhood by abandoning Christianity. As a part of a local Bahá'í community, however, Gregory had been able to weather the storm of criticism. When Alonzo Twine became a Bahá'í in the far more conservative atmosphere of Charleston, he apparently experienced similar opposition, but alone and unable to successfully defend himself. While Twine's case was extreme, it highlighted an important problem for the national Bahá'í movement. During his trip, Gregory had shared the faith directly with some nine hundred people and came away convinced that southern blacks in particular would be "very deeply and vitally interested." He recalled that "people were found who accepted the great Message" in every city that he visited. Yet with only a rudimentary national organization—the annual convention of the Bahai Temple Unity, formed in 1909 to coordinate the building of a Bahá'í House of Worship in Chicago, and its weak executive board—there was no way to assist traveling teachers or keep in touch with widely-scattered seekers and new believers.[18]

AUGUSTA

At about the same time that Louis Gregory was making his first trip through the region, South Carolina received its first permanent Bahá'í resident, who began to build a new local community in Augusta, a metropolitan area straddling the Savannah River between South Carolina and Georgia. A music instructor who had immigrated to New York from Prussia in 1895, Margaret Klebs had first encountered the Bahá'í Faith at the Green Acre summer colony in Maine. By 1911, she was living in South Carolina, when she mailed a contribution from North Augusta to the fund for the proposed Bahá'í House of Worship in Chicago. The following year, interactions with

Margaret Klebs (1862–1939), founder of the local Bahá'í community of Augusta–North Augusta, on the porch of her cabin at Green Acre Bahá'í School, Eliot, Maine, date unknown. Klebs remained closely connected with the mainstream of the American movement in part through summers spent at Green Acre. *Eliot Bahá'í Archives, Eliot, Maine.*

'Abdu'l-Bahá during his visit to the United States helped set the course of her life's work. During a personal meeting, either at Green Acre or in Washington, D.C., 'Abdu'l-Bahá directed Klebs to return to the South to teach the faith. Beginning with the winter of 1912–13 and continuing until the end of her life more than a quarter century later, Klebs spent summers at Green Acre, where lectures, study groups, and interactions with other believers kept her connected to the main currents of American Bahá'í thought and practice, and the remaining nine months or so in the Augusta area, earning a livelihood teaching music classes and individual students. As she got to know her students and their families and staged recitals and concerts to benefit local charities, she attempted to build a new Bahá'í community from scratch. With only a scattering of believers in the entire region, Klebs's arrival represented an additional outpost of the faith in the Deep South.[19]

Likely the first person to introduce the faith in the Augusta area was Louis Gregory, during his 1910 tour of the Southeast. Even so, Klebs's move was a step forward for the faith in both Augusta and the region. Klebs's move provided part of an answer to the question of follow-up that Louis Gregory's foray had raised. By pursuing her livelihood and making friends and acquaintances, Klebs could come in contact with seekers on her own and teach them individually, nurturing a new Bahá'í community through interpersonal contact over an extended period of time. When traveling teachers visited, she could greatly enhance their effectiveness by making arrangements and securing publicity in advance and especially by maintaining contact with those who expressed interest. It was a model that would be repeated in many more locations, in South Carolina and across the United States, in the decades to come.[20]

Klebs's work necessarily put her in close contact with those in the Augusta area who were most able to afford private music instruction and most likely to attend performances of classical music—middle- and upper-class white residents and the wealthy northerners who wintered at the luxury hotels, golf courses, and polo grounds of Aiken and North Augusta—and it was primarily among this segment of the population that she initially attempted to share the Bahá'í message. Early on, she developed a close friendship with the family of James U. Jackson, a wealthy businessman and real estate developer who had built the new garden suburb of North Augusta, South Carolina, just across the river from Augusta. One daughter, Daisy King Jackson, a student of Klebs's, was among the first local people to embrace the faith, and Klebs often staged benefit concerts at the Hampton Terrace Hotel, James Jackson's crowning jewel, a three-hundred-room luxury hotel in North Augusta that was frequented by some of the country's most powerful people. The support of the Jacksons likely lent the Bahá'í Faith an air of legitimacy in the eyes of the public—no small matter in a New South metropolis where white supremacy and religious conservatism were the order of the day.[21]

While Margaret Klebs was able to teach effectively on an individual basis and was comfortable organizing large events, she seems to never have considered herself a public speaker. She therefore relied on outside assistance to attract larger numbers to the faith. In early 1914, she invited Joseph Hannen, Louis Gregory's mentor and one of the strongest proponents of interracial fellowship in the Washington Bahá'í community, to come to the Augusta area for a series of speaking engagements. Hannen's first talk, the evening of March 8, took place at Rosemary Hall, the Jackson mansion in North Augusta. The following night, he was the featured speaker at a concert at the Hampton Terrace to benefit a local children's charity and the Bahá'í Temple project in Chicago. Between sets by Klebs and her students, Hannen addressed an audience of about two hundred people about the faith. Hannen also spoke to students and teachers at the Schofield Normal and Industrial School, an important African American institution in nearby Aiken.[22]

After he returned to Washington, Joseph Hannen reported to 'Abdu'l-Bahá about his trip. 'Abdu'l-Bahá's tablet in reply began by praising Hannen's teaching efforts—particularly the "delivery of an eloquent talk," probably referring to the large gathering at the Hampton Terrace—and assuring him of divine assistance. Then it continued with a prophecy about the future of the Augusta area: "Ere long in that city a great multitude shall enter in the Kingdom of God, the Flag of the oneness of the world of humanity will cast its shade over that state and the Song of the Supreme Concourse will

Hampton Terrace Hotel, North Augusta, postcard circa 1915. The site of Joseph Hannen's "eloquent talk" on the Bahá'í Faith in March 1914, it was the centerpiece of James U. Jackson's dream of a prosperous garden suburb across the Savannah River from Augusta. It burned to the ground in 1916. *South Caroliniana Library, University of South Carolina, Columbia.*

be raised from its glens and dales." Predicting the spiritual transformation of the area, including the growth of the Bahá'í community and the removal of racial prejudice, the letter was as much a confirmation of Klebs's move as it was of Hannen's brief visit, and it inspired her to continue her work in Augusta and North Augusta for another quarter century.[23]

Over the next few years, the area's Bahá'í community grew slowly. At least by the immediate post–World War I years, the little group was sufficiently organized to name delegates to the annual national convention, which helped consolidate the Bahá'í identity of those who attended, and they continued to invite prominent Bahá'ís from other parts of the country to the area. In 1920, for example, Jenabe Assadu'llah Fádil-i-Mazindaráni, an Iranian Bahá'í scholar whom 'Abdu'l-Bahá had sent on a tour of the United States, gave a moving talk about the elimination of prejudice to an audience of "about sixty-five of the [area's] outstanding colored men" at the YMCA. The small community garnered frequent coverage in the local press, and sometimes they were rather bold in their teaching efforts. In January 1917, for example, two believers and a seeker who was a newspaper reporter called on former Populist leader and outspoken white supremacist Thomas E. Watson at his estate in nearby Thomson, Georgia, to share the Bahá'í teachings. According to Margaret Klebs, the "best proof" of the little Bahá'í community's growing influence in the area was that it had been "denounced" from the pulpit in "various churches."[24]

World War I and the Tablets of the Divine Plan

During the years surrounding World War I, Bahá'í teachers across the United States sensed a heightened receptivity to their message, and they worked with more urgency and better coordination than before along several lines at once: teaching the faith and attempting to establish local Bahá'í communities in the South, promoting the Bahá'í vision of interracial unity to broad national audiences, and supporting the work of other emerging interracial organizations in the South and across the country. During the war years, Louis Gregory and other traveling teachers in South Carolina encountered both an African American community that was energized by wartime upheavals to press for full citizenship rights and a tentative new interracial movement that sought to mitigate the worst abuses of the Jim Crow system, and they cultivated important relationships in both areas. They also reported a great deal of receptivity to the faith itself. However, a dearth of permanent Bahá'í settlers and an environment in which wartime activism was brutally suppressed combined to prevent the emergence of new Bahá'í groups outside the Augusta area.

The primary impetus for the upsurge in both teaching and public affairs during the war years came from 'Abdu'l-Bahá. When the Ottoman Empire joined the Central powers in the autumn of 1914, his imprisonment was renewed, and for a period of nearly four years, only a few letters found their way in or out of Haifa and the flow of pilgrims ceased. It was therefore a welcome surprise when, in the summer of 1916, five individuals received tablets from 'Abdu'l-Bahá addressed to the Bahá'ís of the northeastern, central, western, and southern regions of the United States and of Canada, respectively. Published under the title "Tablets of the Divine Plan," they called the believers in North America to spare no effort in spreading their religion to all parts of the continent, directing teachers to travel particularly to those states and provinces where the faith was not established, mentioning the spiritual qualities that the teachers must have, and assuring them of divine assistance. His tablet to the South named all sixteen states in the region as requiring attention. Within a few weeks of the tablets' publication, Joseph Hannen, the secretary of the Washington community's executive body, became the new southern teaching coordinator, and Louis Gregory and two other Washington Bahá'ís were on the road.[25]

Between late October and late December 1916, Louis Gregory visited fourteen of the sixteen states mentioned in the tablet, including South Carolina, speaking mainly in churches, schools, and colleges. Back home in Washington, he reported that during the entire trip, "probably more than fifteen thousand people were reached directly, most of them students, representing many sections and communities." "Without exception," Gregory added, "souls were found ready in cities where the message was given." One significant result of the trip was an invitation to return to Charleston, South Carolina, on January 1, 1917, to deliver the keynote address in the city's Emancipation Day celebration—"an opportunity," he wrote, "to tell them of real freedom." Gregory's speech at Morris Street Baptist Church, part of a daylong program that included a "grand parade" through the city, opened a year of increased activism and self-confidence among blacks across the state. A month after Gregory's speech, James Weldon Johnson, the new field secretary of the NAACP, visited South Carolina as part of his first effort to establish outposts of the organization in the South, and he found people who were ready to act. In Columbia and Charleston, influential black laypeople—many with ties to Avery Institute or otherwise acquaintances of Louis Gregory—took the lead. Gregory had a particularly close, decades-long relationship with two of the founders of the Charleston branch, Edwin A. "Teddy" Harleston, an artist and undertaker, and his sister, Eloise Harleston Jenkins, the wife of a prominent local minister. Both had been students at Avery while Louis Gregory was a teacher there, and they became quite familiar with the Bahá'í Faith from his visits to their home during his trips to the city. Additional branches soon emerged in Aiken, Anderson, Beaufort, Darlington, Florence, and Orangeburg, and by the end of the war, statewide gatherings were issuing bold calls for black political mobilization.[26]

The upsurge of African American activism provoked a violent white reaction, and not just in South Carolina. During and after the war, as more than half a million black southerners migrated to industrial centers in the Northeast and Midwest, white mobs lashed out at black communities across the country. The worst violence came during the "Red Summer" of 1919, when more than two dozen cities and towns, mostly outside the South, erupted in anti-black riots. During the 1920s, a resurgent Ku Klux Klan worked with local and state government officials, law enforcement, and the Federal Bureau of Investigation to destroy the new branches of the NAACP across the South. In South Carolina, the only branches that remained by the middle of the decade were those in Charleston and Columbia, and even they seldom met.[27]

In the wake of the Red Summer, 'Abdu'l-Bahá directed the American Bahá'ís to bring the faith's teachings on interracial unity to the attention of leaders of thought and the general public. Beginning in early 1921 in Washington, where one of the worst riots of 1919 had taken place, the Bahá'ís hosted a series of high-profile conferences aimed at promoting personal contacts across racial lines and dispelling whites' prevailing misinformation about blacks and other racial minorities. Repeated from coast to coast during the rest of the 1920s and 1930s, the conferences and other smaller gatherings involved extensive collaboration with such organizations as the NAACP and the Urban League and a number of progressive intellectuals and religious leaders. At the same time, Louis Gregory and other itinerant teachers in the South made contacts with the Interracial Commission, a network of state and local committees formed in response to the Red Summer that worked to diffuse local racial conflicts and mitigate the worst effects of Jim Crow on black communities. It took a cautiously progressive stance, but in order to maintain a modicum of white support, it remained strongly tied to the region's Protestant establishment and seldom challenged the underlying assumptions of the Jim Crow order. Despite the Interracial Commission's shortcomings, Louis Gregory took its very existence as an improvement, evidence that "many, many souls throughout the South" were "working and longing for a better day." He and other Bahá'ís working in the region sought out the movement's supporters, both to offer encouragement and to seek openings to teach the faith. During a series of trips in South Carolina from 1919 to 1921, for example, Gregory met with Josiah Morse, a professor of philosophy and psychology at the University of South Carolina who was a strong supporter of the state's Interracial Commission. Gregory's positive contact with Morse may have encouraged the latter's interracial activities, which lasted well into the 1930s; it certainly disposed Morse to welcome other Bahá'í teachers to campus in subsequent years.[28]

As the American Bahá'í community was beginning to learn about influencing public discourse about race, an additional intervention by 'Abdu'l-Bahá spurred a further increase in teaching activity. Shortly after the end of World War I, with British forces in control of Palestine and 'Abdu'l-Bahá liberated from house arrest, the Bahá'ís in North America received nine additional Tablets of the Divine Plan that outlined an even more extensive mission than the first set received in 1916. 'Abdu'l-Bahá now called the Bahá'ís in the United States and Canada to spread the faith not only throughout North America but also around the globe. In addition, in a second tablet addressed to the southern states he lamented that "no adequate and befitting motion ha[d] been realized, and no great acclamation and acceleration ha[d] been witnessed" in the region since the introduction of the faith to the United States more than twenty years earlier, and he urged his followers to action. He also indicated that the special mission of the southern Bahá'ís was to overcome the problem of racial prejudice, promising that their efforts would have a transforming impact on the United States and the world.[29]

When the new tablets were presented at the national convention in 1919, the delegates voted to appoint a national Teaching Committee of Nineteen, and Joseph Hannen and Louis Gregory were both among its members. Hannen set up an expanded office, the Central Bureau for the South, charged with distributing literature to seekers and to libraries, publishing articles in the region's newspapers, identifying "all the liberal organizations, clubs, and churches who would be willing to have Bahai lecturers," coordinating teaching circuits and follow-up visits, promoting the establishment of Bahá'í study groups in "all the larger towns," and keeping an index of all the believers in the region. Under the new effort, the number and range of itinerant teachers increased, and Hannen supported them by forwarding mail and financial assistance contributed by other believers. Compared to the virtually nonexistent support network at the time of Louis Gregory's first teaching trip in 1910, it was a major improvement. While Hannen stayed in Washington, Gregory left the convention to begin what would become a nearly three-year period of virtually uninterrupted travel throughout the region, often in tandem with Roy Williams, an African American believer from New York City. The two were particularly active in South Carolina, where Williams later recalled that they "taught together in 30 towns and cities," noting particularly their talks "in many churches in Greenville and Anderson Count[ies]" in the state's Piedmont textile manufacturing belt. Surviving documentation of their engagements during the period is limited, but if Gregory and Williams indeed visited "30 towns and cities" in the relatively compact territory of South Carolina, then their efforts must have touched all parts of the state, including many of the smaller towns.[30]

Despite efforts by Gregory and Williams, it appears that the same forces that suppressed southern branches of the NAACP and kept the Interracial Commission cautious—likely compounded by the fact that no new Bahá'í settlers were forthcoming as in the Augusta area—made it impossible for an indigenous Bahá'í movement to emerge in South Carolina during the wartime years. While visiting teachers found a great deal of receptivity to the faith, one incident indicates that the power of conservative reaction could also be chilling. On the afternoon of Sunday, January 30, 1921, at Sidney Park Colored Methodist Episcopal Church, a fashionable congregation

Reverend Irving E. Lowery (1850–1929), Methodist minister, prolific journalist and writer, advocate of black self-help and accommodation of Jim Crow, and vociferous early opponent of the Bahá'í Faith in South Carolina, circa 1911. *South Caroliniana Library, University of South Carolina, Columbia.*

with an activist minister in downtown Columbia, one of those in attendance was Reverend I.E. Lowery, Alonzo Twine's former minister. After Gregory's talk, Lowery used his regular newspaper column in two black newspapers, the *Watchman and Defender* of Timmonsville and the *Southern Indicator* of Columbia, to denounce him and the religion he espoused. "The [Bahá'í] principles seem to be all right," Lowery warned his readers, "but the Lord Jesus Christ is not recognized in them, and any religion that has no Christ in it, is not worthy of the attention of intelligent Christian people. And any attempt to build up a religion without Christ will be an utter failure." To buttress his point, Lowery recounted the harrowing tale of Alonzo Twine, the "brilliant young lawyer," at his previous church in Charleston, who "took hold of this new religion, and tried to master it," but instead "lost his mind" and died in the insane asylum. Contrary to Lowery's spurious assertions, Gregory and Twine had both become Bahá'ís because they recognized Bahá'u'lláh as the return of Christ, and Gregory's published writings, letters, and talks indicate that he was adept at explaining the new faith in language that was familiar to Christian audiences. Lowery probably attacked the Bahá'í Faith not so much because of its theology but because he felt that its radical teachings on race and its pronounced anti-clericalism might threaten his career as an intermediary between the black community and the white elite. While he was out of step with South Carolina's more progressive black clergymen and an increasingly assertive black community, Lowery's opposition indicates that in South Carolina in the era of the Great War, defenders of the racial order and its Protestant trappings could come in all colors, making the task of Bahá'í community building challenging indeed.[31]

"Organization of the Divine Kingdom"

Planning and Building, 1921–1965

Wﬁith the death of 'Abdu'l-Bahá in 1921, the Bahá'í Faith in the United States entered a new stage of development. Under the direction of his successor Shoghi Effendi, the Guardian of the Cause of God, in little more than a decade the American movement would grow from a loose association of local groups into a closely knit national community with institutions of the faith's emerging brand of spiritual democracy functioning at the local and national levels—a transformation that had a profound effect on the development of the Augusta-area community and on subsequent efforts to establish the faith in other localities in South Carolina. Then, in the mid-1930s, with the Bahá'í administrative system in the United States essentially complete, Shoghi Effendi called the American believers to return in earnest to the global mandate for teaching that 'Abdu'l-Bahá had assigned them in the Tablets of the Divine Plan. The result was a series of multiyear campaigns of expansion and consolidation during which the movement increased its numbers; significantly broadened its geographic scope at home, with a particular focus on the South; and thrust outward into entirely new territory, establishing outposts of the faith and eventually functioning national communities first throughout Latin American and the Caribbean, then in Europe and Africa, and, finally, during a ten-year effort ending in 1963, in virtually all the remaining countries and territories of the globe. During the same period, the Bahá'í Faith in South Carolina grew, despite significant obstacles, into a cohesive statewide movement that far outpaced other religious communities in its commitment to interracial fellowship.

Formative Age

The devastating news of the death of 'Abdu'l-Bahá in November 1921 was soon followed by the instructions he had left in his will for a dual succession to guide the faith into the future. One of the successor institutions was the Universal House of Justice, the international elected body ordained by Bahá'u'lláh in several of his tablets, which would have the power to legislate on matters not explicitly covered in the sacred texts. The other was the Guardianship. Shoghi Effendi, age twenty-four, the eldest grandchild of 'Abdu'l-Bahá and previously his principal English-language secretary, was appointed in the will as "the sign of God, the chosen branch, the Guardian of the Cause of God." After 'Abdu'l-Bahá, he was "the Interpreter of the Word of God," charged with resolving questions of doctrine and ensuring the integrity of the faith's scriptures.[32]

Shoghi Effendi's first concern was the establishment of the Universal House of Justice, but he quickly determined that the conditions specified by 'Abdu'l-Bahá could not immediately be fulfilled. According to the will, secondary or national Houses of Justice should be formed in every country where there were believers, and the members of the secondary Houses of Justice would then "elect the members of the Universal one." But no such institutions yet existed; only the Executive Board of the Bahai Temple Unity in the United States, a relatively weak body, even came close. Moreover, there were only a few dozen rudimentary local bodies, the basis for election of the secondary ones, in the United States and barely a handful in the Middle East. In order to be able to bring the Universal House of Justice into being, then, Shoghi Effendi called on the American community to lead the way in building a proper system of local and national bodies (provisionally designated as "Spiritual Assemblies" to avoid any appearance that the Bahá'ís were attempting to usurp political power) that could then be replicated elsewhere. As Louis Gregory put it in a report of the 1922 national convention, "The time of the organization of the Divine Kingdom on earth ha[d] come."[33]

While the system's founding principles—among them consultation, consensus, and the fundamental unity of the body politic—had already been delineated in the writings of Bahá'u'lláh and 'Abdu'l-Bahá, there were many specific practices and procedures that the Bahá'ís themselves, under Shoghi Effendi's guidance, had to work out. The beginning of the administrative year, for example, was set at the Festival of Ridván (twelve days falling in late April and early May), the anniversary of Bahá'u'lláh's public declaration

SHOUGHI EFFENDI RABBANI
Grandson of His Holiness ABDUL-BAHA

GUARDIAN OF THE
BAHAI CAUSE AND
HEAD OF THE
HOUSE OF JUSTICE

Shoghi Effendi (1897–1957), newly appointed Guardian of the Cause of God, on the cover of the national Bahá'í magazine, January 1922. One of the few American Bahá'ís who had met Shoghi Effendi in person, Louis Gregory fondly recalled from his 1911 pilgrimage "a youth of about fifteen, keenly intelligent, diligent in his work, all reverence and devotion to ['Abdu'l-Bahá]." During his teaching trips around the country, Gregory encouraged his fellow believers to wholeheartedly accept the new institution of the Guardianship. *From* Star of the West.

of his mission in 1863, when elections for the local and national Spiritual Assemblies would be held. The movement's annual national gathering, a tradition since 1909, evolved into the Bahá'í National Convention, which met during Ridván to elect the National Spiritual Assembly and provide it with counsel about the national affairs of the faith. These developments necessitated the maintenance of reliable lists of members and a uniform procedure for enrolling new believers. Voting procedures were refined to ensure the full freedom of the electors, for example, by eliminating the practice of nominations. National and local constitutions and bylaws were adopted, and the National Assembly and strong Local Assemblies secured legal incorporation. The Nineteen Day Feast, a central activity at the roots of the community since the turn of the century, was refined as local groups added a period of consultation between the gathering's devotional and social portions. Through it all, Shoghi Effendi worked to place such details in their proper context, reminding the American community that the "Administrative Order" they were building, during what he termed the faith's "Formative Period" or "Iron Age," was not merely a means to organize one tiny group among all the religions of the world. Rather, he assured them, it was the "nucleus" and "pattern" of the "New World Order" brought by Bahá'u'lláh to revolutionize humanity's collective life. Such a vision helped the Bahá'ís to see their actions, however small, as having potentially far-reaching consequences, enabling individuals raised in a divisive political culture to create a distinctive system of religious governance in little more than a decade.[34]

Teaching and Community Development, 1920s–1930s

During the 1920s and 1930s, Augusta and other localities in South Carolina were both the beneficiaries of and contributors to the developments taking place at the national level. While the development of the Bahá'í administrative structure involved certain elements of centralization and standardization, in the area of teaching, the period was characterized more by decentralization and experimentation. Spurred in part by the financial crisis of the Great Depression, the community developed new teaching methods based on previous successful experiences and learned to involve a larger number of believers in carrying them out. These included the fireside meeting (or simply "fireside"), in which a Bahá'í invited one or more prospective seekers to his or her home, showed hospitality, and discussed some aspect of the faith in an intimate setting. In this way, every believer in a locality could potentially become a confident teacher instead of relying, as the Augusta-area community had, primarily on those who were good public speakers. Another was the study class, which could involve some combination of inquirers, new members, or longtime believers gathering regularly for study of one or more Bahá'í books. Many local communities continued to receive a boost from traveling teachers, but now they could channel those who came to lectures into local firesides and study classes.[35]

All of these approaches were applied in South Carolina, but outside of the Augusta area, the absence of experienced resident believers limited their effectiveness. In 1924, for example, Louis Gregory, who continued unabated his travels after the passing of 'Abdu'l-Bahá, spent twelve days in Sumter, a county seat some sixty miles east of Columbia. He spoke to about 500 students at Morris College, a black Baptist institution; to 1,400 at a black public school; and to smaller audiences at an African Methodist Episcopal church, two white Baptist churches, and a Presbyterian school. Afterward, he reported that there were apparently enough "interested people" in Sumter to form a "small reading circle," but it is unclear whether

Site of Clarence W. Westendorff's oil company, Charleston, 2017. A white Charleston native, Westendorff lived and worked a few blocks from Louis Gregory's family home. When he became a Bahá'í in the early 1920s, he was jailed for preaching the new message on the street. *Author's personal collection.*

the group actually formed or what became of it. From Sumter, he traveled to Charleston, where he spent eight days speaking at five churches, six schools, and two "small interested groups." He also called on Clarence W. Westendorff, a man with whom he had previously corresponded. Westendorff, a white South Carolina native, said that he had embraced the faith based on the literature Gregory had sent him, had begun to preach the message on street corners, and had been jailed as a consequence.

Gregory "advised him not to work in that way, not so melodramatic." After Gregory's visit, Westendorff was listed in Bahá'í membership records and began to receive the national newsletter—an indication of the national community's administrative development since Gregory's first teaching trip in 1910. Yet for some reason Louis Gregory did not recommend the creation of a study group in Charleston as he did in Sumter.[36]

In 1931, a new initiative suggested by Shoghi Effendi and building on previous relationships that Louis Gregory and others had established over the years began sending interracial teams on tours to southern colleges and schools. The first, consisting of Chauncey Northern, a black New Yorker, and Phillip Marangella, an Italian immigrant living in New Hampshire, presented the faith through poetry and song in Virginia and the Carolinas. In Columbia, they visited with white students at the University of South Carolina and black students at Allen University and Benedict College, Reconstruction-era black institutions in the heart of the city's principal black middle-class neighborhood. In Orangeburg, they visited two more black institutions, Claflin University and the Colored Normal, Industrial, Agricultural, and Mechanical College (or "State College," the future South Carolina State University). They reported finding receptive audiences of "theologians and students" in Orangeburg, where several people recalled "previous visits of other teachers of the Bahá'í Cause" (probably Louis Gregory and Roy Williams) and one dean said that he would start a Bahá'í study group "as soon as literature was received for it." As in Sumter, however, it is unclear what became of the group.[37]

In the Augusta area, where there was already a small group of resident believers, the new approaches in the 1920s and early 1930s bore more fruit than elsewhere in South Carolina. In March 1934, Stanwood Cobb, a prominent educator in the Washington, D.C. area, visited to conduct a "teaching campaign," a series of public lectures aimed at starting a study group. The local Bahá'ís arranged for at least seven talks in Augusta and North Augusta, and after the visit there were enough interested people that some of the seekers and veteran believers started a study group at the home of one of the seekers, Marie Kershaw, the area's only female physician, in North Augusta. For more than a year, some fifteen to twenty-five people, a virtual cross section of white Augusta-area society, met weekly to study a series of Bahá'í texts, and Kershaw and a number of the other participants quickly embraced the faith. At Ridván 1935, the newly enlarged community gathered at Kershaw's house to elect its Local Spiritual Assembly. Of the nine inaugural members, two were longtime Bahá'ís and seven new; five

Zia Mabsut Bagdadi (1884–1937), physician, editor, lecturer, administrator, energetic proponent of interracial unity, and member of one of the oldest Arab Bahá'í families who was brought up in Bahá'u'lláh's household. When Bagdadi died suddenly in Augusta, Shoghi Effendi called the loss to the "national interests" of the faith "irreparable." *National Bahá'í Archives.*

lived in North Augusta and four in Augusta. It was the first Local Spiritual Assembly anywhere in the Carolinas and Georgia.[38]

By 1937, the Augusta-area community numbered more than thirty members, with perhaps at least that many regular friends and seekers participating in activities. At least two of the members were African American women, but it appears that the local community was only partially integrated. Surviving records indicate that some of the white believers visited the black believers in their homes to pray and study together, but blacks may have been functionally excluded when activities took place in the homes of whites or in public spaces. The person who came closest to setting the Augusta-area community on a more firmly interracial basis was Zia Bagdadi. An immigrant from Palestine who had pursued medical studies in Chicago, he was a well-known editor and administrator in the national Bahá'í movement and an energetic proponent of interracial fellowship in the Chicago community. Late in 1936, after first visiting the area as a traveling teacher, Bagdadi moved to Augusta with his family, opened a medical practice, and immediately set out to bring the faith to larger numbers of African Americans. The most promising opening was among working-class African Americans in North Augusta, at the home of Marie Kershaw's washerwoman. As Kershaw recalled, "Zia made Thursday evening talks to first a handful of colored friends…then to a houseful, then to a house and porch and yard full, and then to a tremendous gathering." The meetings ended abruptly, however. "Evidently the authorities were displeased with such large groups of colored people gathering," Kershaw wrote, "because after this the house became dark and closed to us." When Bagdadi died suddenly in April 1937, barely six months after his arrival, the community was left without its one potential champion of teaching African Americans.[39]

The First Seven Year Plan (1937–1944)

In the late 1930s, with the basic features of the Bahá'í administrative system in place, Shoghi Effendi was ready to relaunch the community on the mission of spreading the faith worldwide that 'Abdu'l-Bahá had outlined in the Tablets of the Divine Plan. The first Seven Year Plan, begun in 1937 against the backdrop of persistent economic distress and a world careening toward the outbreak of another major war, had two main objectives: completion of the elaborate exterior ornamentation of the Bahá'í Temple in Wilmette, a northern suburb of Chicago—the massive concrete-and-steel superstructure had been completed during the terrible early years of the Great Depression—and establishment of Local Spiritual Assemblies in all the remaining states and provinces of North America and in every republic and major island of Latin America and the Caribbean. It was a daunting undertaking. In particular, the plan's ambitious geographic goals would require both a major movement of the American Bahá'í population and a more active engagement by the rank and file of the community. From previous experience of attempting to extend into new areas, including South Carolina, it was clear that only the "settlement plan," in which individuals or families from established Bahá'í communities would settle as "pioneers" in each of the plan's "virgin territories," would be sufficient.[40]

In addition to formidable logistical challenges, the plan heralded significant cultural and demographic change, as a national community that was still mostly white, northern, and urban turned a great deal of its attention toward the South. Nearly thirty years after a handful of Bahá'ís had taken up residence on the edges of the region—in Baltimore, Washington, and the Gulf Coast radical colony of Fairhope, Alabama—the South accounted for twelve of the twenty-six virgin territories in North America. Only six cities south of the Potomac—Augusta; Nashville and Memphis, Tennessee; Tuskegee, Alabama; and Miami and St. Augustine, Florida—had enough Bahá'ís to form a Local Spiritual Assembly, and five of the sixteen southern states had no believers at all. While the movement already had some experience building interracial local communities in the South and elsewhere, and Louis Gregory and other traveling teachers had been nurturing positive contacts with progressive individuals and groups, black and white, across the region for years, few American Bahá'ís were really ready to confront the challenges of establishing the faith in the heart of Jim Crow's pervasive segregation and violence. Suddenly, the challenges faced by the early Washington and Augusta communities would be repeated simultaneously in multiple localities at once, forcing the national community to confront some of the ugliest realities of American racism on a far larger scale than ever before.[41]

In preparation for the start of the Seven Year Plan, Shoghi Effendi urged the community to manifest complete and uncompromising interracial fellowship—a theme he had repeated consistently since the beginning of his ministry. The outline of a southern teaching policy emerged in 1936 in conjunction with a visit by the National Spiritual Assembly to the nascent local community in Nashville. While Shoghi Effendi insisted on the holding of a number of interracial public meetings in Nashville—at least a "foot in the door" of segregation, as one black Nashville believer recalled—he acknowledged that in some localities teaching activities such as firesides and study classes might need to be conducted separately for black and white seekers. However, he insisted that the local community's internal functions—including the Nineteen Day Feast, observances of the faith's Holy Days, and elections for and membership on the Local Spiritual Assembly—could brook no compromise with segregation, regardless of the possible dangers of holding integrated gatherings. In December 1938, he issued a book-length letter, published as *The Advent of Divine Justice*, that made the faith's commitment to interracial unity unmistakable. Offering a cogent arraignment of American materialism and its manifestations in white supremacy, widespread political and economic inequality, and moral decay, he called the problem of unexamined racial prejudice "the most vital and challenging issue confronting the Bahá'í community at this stage of its existence." He warned that not only the success of the Seven Year Plan but ultimately the destiny of the American nation depended upon the extent to which the Bahá'ís were able to build "an interracial fellowship completely purged from the curse of racial prejudice." The work provided binding terms of reference—and a challenging standard—for a movement seeking to establish itself in the strongholds of the Jim Crow order.[42]

New Footholds in South Carolina

During the course of the plan, pioneers settled in South Carolina's three largest cities: Charleston, Columbia, and Greenville. The first to arrive, in December 1937, were Emogene Hoagg and Agnes O'Neill, financially independent white women, who spent the winter in Charleston. Others followed them, usually for a few months at a time, over the next few years. Hoagg returned in 1939 and worked to establish a study group with little success. One person she contacted was Clarence Westendorff, whom she found had drifted away from the faith in more than a decade of isolation and whose neighbors considered him to be "erratic." More promising were contacts with her landlady, who invited Hoagg to speak to her chapter of the Daughters of the King, a women's order affiliated with the Episcopal Church; with a Unitarian minister, who invited her to his church's Women's Alliance; and with "the colored Librarian," probably Susan Dart Butler, founder of the city's first library open to African Americans, who invited Hoagg to speak on the faith to friends in her home and included Bahá'í books in the library's collection. After less than a year, however, Hoagg was requested to move to Havana, Cuba, to help fulfill a plan goal there, and no study group emerged in Charleston.[43]

More successful were the pioneers who moved to Columbia. From 1938 through the early 1940s, Maude Mickle and Alta Wheeler, single white women from Maine, began spending the winter months in Columbia and were able to lay the foundations of a new local community. Louella Moore, a white woman who had first learned about the faith in North Augusta, became a Bahá'í shortly after meeting Mickle and Wheeler. Another contact, Pearl Dixon, the widow of an African Methodist Episcopal minister, arranged for the pioneers to speak at her home and embraced the faith immediately. Her grown daughter, Jessie Entzminger, was more hesitant. "I had never heard tell of the Bahá'í Faith," Entzminger recalled. "It sounded like a funny name." Nevertheless, she joined the new study group that began meeting in her mother's home and became a Bahá'í six months later. Over the next several years, at least two African American traveling teachers, Louis Gregory and Zenobia Dorsey of Scranton, Pennsylvania, visited Columbia to assist the small group. During Dorsey's visits in 1942 and 1943, for example, she spoke to the Waverly Friendship Club, a women's social and service organization in the neighborhood surrounding Allen University and Benedict College; three of the club's members became Bahá'ís, and a number of others joined the ongoing study class at Pearl Dixon's house. The Columbia community also used the local press, black and white, to advertise its aims and activities.[44]

The source of the first pioneers to Greenville was much closer to home. William and Christine Bidwell, whites from Tennessee and South Carolina, respectively, had first learned of the faith while living in Florida and become Bahá'ís as part of the first study group in North Augusta. In the

Louis Gregory with Bahá'ís and friends, Columbia, circa 1940s. *Left to right*: Celia Glenn, Lutie McKim, Alta Wheeler, Ethel Lowery, Louis Gregory, Eunice Long, Louella Moore, Jessie Entzminger, and Mrs. Carroll. During the 1940s and 1950s, Columbia's small Bahá'í community was centered in the middle-class black neighborhood of Waverly. *Columbia Bahá'í Archives, Columbia, South Carolina.*

spring of 1938, they moved to Greenville, a major textile center not far from Christine's family home of Pendleton in Anderson County. They bought a large house downtown, where William, a chiropractor and naturopathic physician, also opened an office to see patients. Soon, they had a number of contacts for teaching, but there were no new believers. In 1942, with the end of the Seven Year Plan less than two years away, the Regional Teaching Committee of the Carolinas and Georgia, a subsidiary of the National Teaching Committee created early in the plan, selected Greenville as the state's goal city for the formation of a Local Spiritual Assembly, and several new short-term pioneers arrived. Two local white women soon embraced the faith, Virginia Ford, who was at home with her young daughter while her husband was away in the war, and Carolyn Glazener, a businesswoman who had been studying for some time with the Bidwells. In 1943, Roy and Bernice Williams, an African American couple from New York, arrived with intentions to stay indefinitely. Roy Williams was already familiar with the area, having visited Greenville with Louis Gregory during their extended travels of 1919–21. Both of their professions—he opened a fine furniture restoration shop and she taught French at the area's only black high school—afforded them ample opportunities to get to know people in their new community. Greenville's

Local Spiritual Assembly—the first in South Carolina beyond Augusta–North Augusta—was finally established in November 1943, only a few months shy of the end of the plan. With the Williamses as members, it reflected the tiny group's tentatively interracial character.[45]

In May 1944, with war still raging in Europe and Asia, the National Spiritual Assembly hosted a special All-America Convention in Chicago to mark both the centenary of the Declaration of the Báb (the announcement of his prophetic mission to his first disciple) and what Shoghi Effendi termed the community's "total victory" in the Seven Year Plan. Honorary delegates from Latin America joined some 1,600 believers from the United States and Canada—fully one-third of the movement's members in North America—including Louella Moore and Roy and Bernice Williams from South Carolina. One of the speakers hailed the convention as "the highest type of democracy" and the diversity of the participants as proof "that human nature can change, that new social values can deliberately be created." In view of the long-term development of the religion around the world, the presence of black and white believers from Columbia and Greenville—part of a cohesive interracial Bahá'í movement that now spanned the South—was perhaps as significant as that of the representatives from Latin America.[46]

Participants in the All-America Convention on the steps of the Bahá'í House of Worship, Wilmette, Illinois, May 1944. The largest gathering of Bahá'ís in the Western Hemisphere up to that time, it included representatives from new outposts of the faith in Latin America as well black and white believers from Columbia, Greenville, and other Deep South cities. The crystalline quartz for the innovative cast-concrete exterior of the House of Worship was mined near Spartanburg, South Carolina. *Author's personal collection.*

The Second Seven Year Plan (1946–1953)

In 1946, after what Shoghi Effendi called a "two-year respite" while the dust of war settled, the North American Bahá'ís launched a second seven-year campaign focused on strengthening the administrative foundations of the faith in the Americas and establishing new communities in Africa and Europe. In South Carolina, the plan was essentially a time of consolidation. Benefiting from an effective regional committee structure that coordinated resources across the Carolinas and Georgia, the South Carolina community worked to increase the size and diversity of its membership, use the mass media to address postwar concerns and attract public attention, and establish a new Local Spiritual Assembly in Columbia (in 1949). By the end of the plan, there were only a few more than thirty Bahá'ís in South Carolina, but they were already a virtual microcosm of the state. Two-thirds of the believers were natives who had embraced the faith locally; the proportion of blacks and whites reflected the racial composition of the general population; and they spanned the range of social, economic, and educational status from domestics to textile mill workers to scions of the antebellum elite.[47]

The community's diversity was certainly hard-won. Early in the second Seven Year Plan, neighbors called the police to break up an integrated meeting at the home of Marie Kershaw, who had moved from North Augusta to Columbia to work in a new veterans' hospital. After that, the Columbia Bahá'ís only met in the homes of black believers and seekers or in rented halls. In Greenville, where a long history of black and labor activism had frequently provoked violent suppression, indiscreet comments by some of the pioneers apparently brought accusations of communism—a common charge against any southern organization pursuing an interracial agenda—and an investigation by the FBI that caused new believer Carolyn Glazener to distance herself from the community. When black believers and seekers came to the homes of white Bahá'ís, they often entered discreetly through the back door so as not to arouse the suspicion of neighbors. Even so, the Ku Klux Klan burned a cross on Virginia Ford's front lawn after black Bahá'ís visited.

Greenville Bahá'ís, circa 1950s. Pictured here are, from left to right (*front*): Grace von der Heidt, Roy Williams, unidentified, unidentified; (*back*) Bernice Williams, unidentified, unidentified, Virginia Ford, William Bidwell, and Christine Bidwell. The Greenville community struggled for more than a decade to find safe spaces for interracial public gatherings. *National Bahá'í Archives.*

For more than a decade, the community struggled to find public venues that would accommodate interracial meetings, finally turning to the mayor, who arranged for the Bahá'ís to use city council chambers for the purpose. Just before the end of the plan in early 1953, Roy Williams appeared before the city council to ask for a formal acknowledgement of the community's interracial character and protection for its activities. The council decided that interracial religious gatherings did not violate city ordinances and that the Bahá'ís "could not be interfered with…because of the guarantee of freedom of worship." While the ruling hardly ended the Bahá'ís' difficulties, either in Greenville or Columbia, it was an important step toward securing recognition of the faith by the state government.[48]

The Ten Year Plan (1953–1963)

As the second Seven Year Plan came to a close, Shoghi Effendi announced an immediate start to a new and even more challenging endeavor: all of the twelve existing National Spiritual Assemblies would cooperate in a "fate-laden, soul-stirring, decade-long, world-embracing Spiritual Crusade" to establish the faith in all the remaining countries of the world. The specific tasks of the Ten Year Plan staggered the imagination: some 250 territories would require pioneers; the number of National Spiritual Assemblies would be more than quadrupled; scores of national headquarters and other properties would be purchased; and two new Houses of Worship, in Tehran, Iran, and Frankfurt, West Germany, would be built. At the World Center of the faith, construction of the International Bahá'í Archives, the first of a series of administrative buildings that Shoghi Effendi envisioned on the slope of Mount Carmel, would begin. The plan's culmination would come at Riḍván 1963, the centenary of Bahá'u'lláh's declaration of his prophetic mission to the followers of the Báb, when believers from around the world would gather in a World Congress—initially planned for Baghdad, the site of the original Festival of Riḍván, but moved to London due to considerable opposition to the faith in Iraq—to celebrate their achievements. The lion's share of the international goals would fall to the United States. In addition, the American community's domestic goals included building extensive gardens around the newly completed Temple in Chicago, nearly doubling the number of Local Spiritual Assemblies (from 171 to 300), extending the national public-relations campaign using the mass media, and initiating the community's first systematic outreach to Native Americans. After the unexpected death of Shoghi Effendi midway through the plan in late 1957, the Hands of the Cause of God, a special cadre of deputies he had appointed to assist with the expansion and consolidation of the faith, assumed temporary custody of the community's international affairs. The Hands soon added another goal: at the end of the plan in 1963, all the National Spiritual Assemblies then in existence would participate in an election to establish the Universal House of Justice.[49]

In South Carolina, the Ten Year Plan began with the Bahá'í community in straitened circumstances. In contrast to the previous two plans, which had taken place in the context of the relative racial moderation of the New Deal and World War II, the mid-1950s witnessed a fresh campaign by state and local officials and white citizens' groups to dismantle the NAACP. Brought on by *Briggs v. Elliott*, the Clarendon County school desegregation case that was winding its way to the U.S. Supreme Court, and wrapped up in the anticommunist fervor of the Cold War, the campaign of suppression made the Bahá'ís' interracialism more dangerous than usual, and during the early years of the plan, the statewide community could do little more than hold itself together. During the early 1960s, however, as the civil rights movement began to register more gains and the state's political and business elite attempted to ease the transition to desegregation, the legal, social, and economic risks of identifying with an interracial movement—to both blacks and whites—began to soften somewhat. With the arrival of a few energetic new pioneers, the Bahá'í community drew dozens of new members, established new outposts in the state's rural Black Belt, and became more outspoken in its public support for civil rights.

In 1956, spurred by repeated appeals from Shoghi Effendi to broaden the foundations of the faith at home, particularly in the South and among African Americans, Joy Faily Benson of Michigan applied for medical residency at Greenville General Hospital. When she and her husband, Richard, an attorney who was not yet a Bahá'í, arrived in Greenville, they found only a few believers left in the city. The Bahá'ís' reputation for religious and racial radicalism, however, was strong enough that when the prestigious law firm that Richard Benson applied to found out that he was associated with them, he was turned down for the job and blacklisted from other firms. The Bensons received threatening phone calls and became the subject of wild rumors, and their children were harassed. Police shined their headlights at the Bensons' front door to see who was coming and going at their house, and a neighbor who was a state legislator circulated a petition to the General

Assembly alleging that the Bahá'ís were communists and illicit race-mixers. Despite opposition, the Bensons and Joy's parents, who followed them to Greenville, persisted in making social connections with African Americans and sharing the faith with them.[50]

In 1960, one black teenager the Bensons met, Richard Abercrombie, came to a fireside where the speaker was Eulalia Barrow Bobo, a traveling teacher from California who was a sister of the boxing champion Joe Louis Barrow. He was so impressed with Bobo's explanation of the faith that he embraced it immediately. His parents, Charles and Lillie Abercrombie, were staunch Baptists and skeptical at first, but in short order, they, too, became Bahá'ís. When they began to advertise Bahá'í meetings at their house, Charles Abercrombie's work as a building contractor quickly dried up, and they took it as a chance to go on the road to teach the faith to other family members in Tennessee and Michigan. Within the year, most of the rest of the family, including all of their children, two of Charles's brothers, and Lillie's mother in Michigan, had embraced the faith. It was the first time in South Carolina that an entire extended family had become Bahá'ís. There was a steady stream of new believers in addition to the Abercrombies, including school friends of the Abercrombie children and a white retired textile mill worker and members of his family. Almost overnight, the decades-long problem of having enough believers to maintain the Local Spiritual Assembly was solved, and by 1962, there were even enough outside the city limits to form the first Local Assembly of Greenville County. At the same time, the Greenville community took two steps to ensure greater legal protection for the faith in South Carolina: in 1961, they asked for and received an opinion of the state's attorney general that permitted Local Spiritual Assemblies to perform marriages, and the following year, the Local Assembly of Greenville secured legal incorporation.[51]

In addition to a revitalized community in Greenville, the late 1950s and early 1960s saw the emergence of new outposts of the faith in rural, black-majority areas of South Carolina. In January 1957, new Bahá'ís Jordan and Annette Young, recently married, white, and from Massachusetts and Georgia, respectively, moved with their infant son to Florence, the largest town in the Pee Dee River basin in the eastern corner of the state. Graduates of Palmer College of Chiropractic in Iowa, they soon opened an office where they planned for all their patients to use a single entrance. Instead, they found that only whites came. In order to attract black patients, they had to cut another door in the back and install a "colored entrance in rear" sign, but inside, they maintained one waiting

Greenville Bahá'ís and friends with visitors from Augusta, Phillis Wheatley Center, 1962. Richard Abercrombie and his mother, Lillie Abercrombie (1921–2016), members of the first extended family to become Bahá'ís in South Carolina, are seated front row *(first and second from left, respectively)*. *Personal collection of Joy F. Benson.*

room and used two treatment rooms interchangeably for black and white patients. Their practice grew quickly, and as the only chiropractors in the area, they soon had patients driving from as far away as Myrtle Beach. Gradually they began to invite some to the office after hours for firesides; several black patients from Florence and Myrtle Beach, as well as their white receptionist and her husband, embraced the faith. In 1961, another white couple, native South Carolinians Lee and Genelle Grimsley, who had also learned of the faith at Palmer, settled in Lake City, a small town in the southern part of Florence County. They soon attracted a handful of new believers through their practice and began holding social activities and Bahá'í classes for African American children and youth. There were enough Bahá'ís to form a Local Spiritual Assembly in the city of Florence in 1961 and in Florence County the following year.

Around the same time, the Southeastern Bahá'í Schools Committee, which ran weeklong summer and winter residential programs of study, arts, and socializing, stopped using a YMCA camp in North Carolina when the management complained that there were "too many" blacks in attendance. Instead, the committee secured the use of Penn Center, formerly one of the first schools for freedpeople in the South, on black-majority St. Helena Island at the southern tip of South Carolina. During the 1961–62 winter school session, the committee arranged for Eulalia Barrow Bobo to give an Emancipation Day speech at Brick Baptist Church, the oldest congregation on the island, resulting in additional meetings in the home of a local resident and a handful of new believers. By 1963, there were enough Bahá'ís on the island to form a Local Spiritual Assembly.[52]

In Greenville, a larger, more diverse, and more legally secure local Bahá'í community became more confident in upholding social equality in its public and private activities, more creative in its outreach activities, and

Eight members of the first Local Spiritual Assembly of Florence, 1961. Pictured here are, from left to right (*front*): unidentified, Otis Williams, and Robert Bacote; (*middle*) Almetta Player and Fannie Williams; (*back*) David Jurney, Mattie Bacote, and Paul Bacote. The Local Spiritual Assemblies of Florence and of St. Helena Island represented a major step in establishing the Bahá'í Faith in South Carolina's Black Belt. *Florence Bahá'í Archives, Florence, South Carolina.*

SOUTHEASTERN
BAHÁ'Í
SUMMER SCHOOL
FROGMORE, S.C.

SO. CAROLINA
BEAUFORT
BAHÁ'Í SCHOOL SOUTHEASTERN

AUGUST 13-19 1960

Above: Some of the participants in the Southeastern Bahá'í Summer School, Penn Center, St. Helena Island, July 1961. Penn Center, formerly a school for freedpeople, was one of the few places in the region during the early 1960 that would host the Bahá'ís' integrated seasonal conferences. *Personal collection of Joy F. Benson.*

Left: Brochure for Southeastern Bahá'í Summer School, Penn Center, St. Helena Island, 1960. *Personal collection of Joy F. Benson.*

Opposite: Newspaper advertisement for Spiritual Singing Convention, Greenville, September 1964. The ad includes quotations from both the "Negro National Anthem" and the writings of Bahá'u'lláh. The local Bahá'í community's participation was a strong statement of support for the civil rights movement. *From the* Greenville (SC) News.

COME!

LIFT EVERY VOICE AND SING!
LIFT EVERY HEART IN PRAYER!

SPIRITUAL SINGING CONVENTION

A CONVENTION FOR AMITY.

Featured Groups — Co-directed by Mrs. Othie Reeder and Mrs. Helen Donald.

Mrs. Ethel Waters at the organ.

New World Singers of Washington, D. C., starring "Skip" Hackenbury
Master James Howard Donald—Guest Soloist
The Bland Sisters
A Surprise Twelve Year Old Prodigy Soloist of Charleston
Youth Singers of Greenville
Invincible Five of Greenville
Friendly Six of Piedmont
Mt. Calvary Junior Gospel
The Christian Travelers Gospel Singers
The Three Stars
The Crusaders
Stop Light Gospel Singers
The Silver Stars
Gethsemane Gospel Singers
St. Paul Gospel Singers
Junior Gospel Singers of Tabernacle Baptist
Queen Street Gospel Singers
Pleasant View Gospel Singers
Friendship Singing Class
New Zion Holiness Singers, Seniors and Juniors
The Evangelistic Gospel Singers
Lowndes Hill Gospel Singers
Mt. Zion Gospel Singers
The Roulettes of Laurens
Christian Travelers Gospel
The Golden Voices of Travelers Rest
Blue Ridge Gospel Singers
Heavenly Gospel Singers
Congregational Baptist
Mt. View Holiness Gospel Chorus
Enoree Juniors
Heart Teachers
Standard Gospel Singers
The Waters Gospel Group
Rev. Benny Campbell and Pianist

Also Group Singing led by Doug Ruhe of Wilmette, Illinois (a student at Kansas University)

Featured Speakers:

Matthew Perry of Columbia
Dr. William Tucker of Asheville
Rev. James Bevel, S. C. L. C. of Atlanta
Mrs. Mary Lee Davis of Charleston
Rev. D. S. Francis, Springfield Baptist Church, Moderator

SPONSORED BY:

John Bolt Culbertson

"Ye are the fruits of one tree and the leaves of one branch."

"So powerful is the light of unity that it can illumine the whole world."

John Bolt Culbertson

SUNDAY SEPT. 20th.

DOORS OPEN AT 1:30 P. M.

Greenville Memorial Auditorium

Greenville, S. C.

ADMISSION FREE to ALL!

more vocal in its support for the mainstream civil rights movement. During the late 1950s and early 1960s, the Greenville community regularly hosted interracial picnics, study groups, Holy Day observances, and other public programs that included their non-Bahá'í classmates, friends, and family members, as well as prominent activists. During 1963 and 1964, the community took a public stand in a protracted controversy over the desegregation of city pools, with individual Bahá'ís speaking at city council meetings and appearing in the local press. During a summer youth project in 1964, local and visiting Bahá'ís, black and white, worked with Springfield Baptist Church, a prominent black congregation, to tutor the first group of African American students who would attend all-white schools that fall under a court-ordered desegregation plan. That September, they helped host the Spiritual Singing Convention—sponsored by local labor and civil rights attorney John Bolt Culbertson—at Memorial Auditorium, the city's premier concert venue. Two of the thirty-five musical groups, drawn mostly from local black churches, were made up of Bahá'ís, and the speakers included Matthew Perry of Spartanburg, attorney for the state conference of the NAACP; veteran activist Reverend James Bevel of the Southern Christian Leadership Conference in Atlanta, representing Dr. Martin Luther King Jr.; and Dr. William Tucker, a white Bahá'í from Asheville, North Carolina. For a small local Bahá'í community that had almost disappeared in the anti–civil rights repression of the late 1950s, these were bold statements of alliance with the black freedom struggle.[53]

Greenville Bahá'ís and friends, Phillis Wheatley Community Center, April 1964. *Personal collection of Joy F. Benson.*

Furman University chapter of Southern Student Organizing Committee (SSOC), Greenville, 1968. Joseph Vaughn (1946–1991, *second from right*), a Greenville Bahá'í who was the first black undergraduate to attend a historically white private college in South Carolina, became a teacher in the Greenville County public schools. June Manning Thomas (*second from left*), daughter of NAACP leaders in Orangeburg, associated with Bahá'ís in Greenville while a student at Furman, embraced the faith later, and eventually became a professor of urban planning at the University of Michigan. *Special Collections, James B. Duke Library, Furman University.*

One of the new believers in Greenville found himself in the spotlight of the local movement. In January 1965, Joseph Vaughn, a star graduate of Sterling High School and veteran of Greenville's sit-in protests who had been associating with the Bahá'ís for two years, was admitted to Furman University, becoming the state's first black undergraduate student at a historically white private university. He excelled academically at Furman and continued his activism, most notably as vice-president of the campus chapter of the Southern Student Organizing Committee, an affiliate of Students for a Democratic Society. June Manning (later Thomas), a black Orangeburg native who enrolled at Furman in 1967, recalled that Vaughn "used humor and silliness" to cope with the stress of having been the university's first black student. He likely faced difficulties as a religious minority as well. During his junior year, Vaughn wrote in defense of his new faith for the Baptist school's student newspaper. Its goal, he stated, was "to revitalize mankind spiritually, break down barriers between peoples, and lay foundations for a unified world based on unity and love."[54]

Vaughn's words reflected the intersection of Bahá'í teachings and practices with Martin Luther King's ideal of the "beloved community," a transformed and spiritualized society characterized by justice, love, and the "total interrelatedness" of all people. Indeed, by the time the civil rights movement reached its apogee in the mid-1960s, the tiny Bahá'í community, with branches in several cities and smaller towns and an unusually diverse body of members, probably came closer to fulfilling King's vision than any other religious group in the state. However, the Bahá'ís' small numbers severely limited their ability to effect the wholesale transformation of society anticipated by Bahá'u'lláh and for which enlightened leaders such as King were increasingly calling. That situation would begin to change during the next decade.[55]

"Let Nothing Stop Us"

Becoming a Mass Movement, 1963–1973

While the Baháʼís in South Carolina in the early 1960s were no doubt familiar with the many passages in the writings of their faith that anticipated substantial growth in the future, nothing in the previous half century had prepared them for the transformation that would take place with the rapid decline of Jim Crow. As formal racial barriers buckled across the South and increasing signs of political chaos gripped the country, the Universal House of Justice continued Shoghi Effendi's pattern of global teaching plans, directing the Baháʼís in every country to bring the message of the faith to the masses of their fellow citizens as never before. The impulse for growth coming from within the Baháʼí Faith thus met the heightened social and spiritual concerns of American society at large. The result was a dramatic growth in membership, particularly among young people and racial minorities, that permanently altered the character, organization, and aspirations of the Baháʼí movement in the United States. The epicenter of this development was South Carolina.

The Nine Year Plan and the "Masses of Mankind"

Just six months after its formation in April 1963, the Universal House of Justice began to set out its vision for the next stage of the religion's development. In a letter to the world's National Spiritual Assemblies, the new head of the faith wrote pointedly that while the previous decade's labors had resulted in a giant leap forward in terms of global reach, in order for the community to "extend its influence into all strata of society," it would need to "grow rapidly in size." With the framework of the Administrative Order essentially complete and established in virtually every country, the Universal House of Justice called for a "huge expansion of the Cause of God" during a new Nine Year Plan set to start in 1964. Recalling the world-historical implications of mass conversions to Christianity and Islam in centuries past, a second major message in July 1964 outlined a detailed strategy for teaching among the "masses of mankind." Based on the experience of several national communities, primarily in Africa and Asia, during the previous decade, the House of Justice now said that every National Assembly should begin to direct its attention to "village areas" as much as it previously had to "cities and towns," "so balanc[ing] its resources and harmoniz[ing] its efforts that the Faith of God is taught not only to those who are readily accessible but to all sections of society, however remote they may be." While in most countries the previous experience of teaching had been limited to a trickle of individual seekers and new believers, primarily in cities, the vision of the House of Justice focused on the movement of entire populations toward the faith. In this context, the House of Justice clarified that people "need not know all the proofs, history, laws, and principles of the Faith" before being enrolled as believers. Rather, becoming a Bahá'í should be viewed as a "process." "[I]n addition to catching the spark of faith," new believers should "become basically informed about the Central Figures of the Faith, as well as the existence of laws they must follow and an administration they must obey." After declaration of faith came an indefinite period of consolidation: "Through correspondence and dispatch of visitors, through conferences and training courses, these friends must be patiently strengthened and lovingly helped to develop into full Bahá'í maturity."[56]

The new approach described by the Universal House of Justice implied a substantial revision of the way most national communities deployed their human and financial resources. In the United States, it also heralded a revision in the community's very definition of itself. While the faith had spread relatively early to a few rural outposts, including in the South, the urban centers of the North and the West Coast had long dominated the American Bahá'í community. As recently as the Ten Year Plan, Shoghi Effendi had implored—largely in vain—the believers in New York, Chicago, and other large cities to disperse to fulfill homefront pioneering goals in smaller localities. Even in South Carolina, a state with a population that was still mostly rural, the emergence of new local communities in places as small as Florence, Lake City, and St. Helena Island was the exception, not the rule. As in the previous plan, during the early years of the Nine Year Plan, the American community sent out the majority of international pioneers, while a series of ambitious domestic goals—including doubling of the number of Local Spiritual Assemblies (to six hundred) and specific teaching efforts aimed at minority groups—proceeded more slowly. Even so, between 1963 and 1968, the Bahá'í population of the United States grew by more than one third, from eleven thousand to nearly eighteen thousand. Significantly, most of the new believers were teenagers and young adults, with college campuses increasingly becoming centers of Bahá'í activity. By the end of the decade, spurred by increasing social and political upheaval and by additional guidance from the Universal House of Justice, the influx of young people would make itself felt in dramatic fashion in the Deep South.[57]

Darkness and Light

In October 1967, the Universal House of Justice added an even more pointed note of urgency to the work of the Nine Year Plan. Inaugurating a two-year global public relations campaign to commemorate the centenary of Bahá'u'lláh's proclamation of his mission to the monarchs and ecclesiastics of his own time, the House of Justice told the Bahá'ís to expect an immediate future of increasing chaos. When the political and religious leaders of the late nineteenth century had rejected Bahá'u'lláh's counsels, it explained, humanity had been granted a "hundred-year respite." Now, the House of Justice announced, the respite appeared to have come to an end. The world was entering "the dark heart of this age of transition"—a harrowing prediction considering the record of suffering during the previous hundred years. Such predictions certainly seemed apt in the United States, where the late 1960s witnessed a rising tide of urban uprisings, polarization over the war in Vietnam, a rash of political assassinations, and dramatic political realignments. But the House of Justice did not counsel despair. Amid the deepening gloom, the Bahá'ís would find new opportunities to extend the influence of the faith: "Sustained by our love for each other and given power through the Administrative Order…the Army of Light can achieve such victories as will astonish posterity."[58]

For the Bahá'ís in South Carolina, there were encouraging developments across the state during the final years of the decade. During 1967 and 1968, pioneers moved to Winnsboro, the seat of Fairfield County north of Columbia, and Rock Hill, a textile town just south of Charlotte, and new communities began to emerge in both places. In the Columbia area, growth was robust enough for the establishment of a new Local Spiritual Assembly in Richland County and a Bahá'í student organization at historically black Benedict College, both in 1969. A Bahá'í community finally began to emerge in Charleston when a young white man who had become a Bahá'í while serving in the navy returned to his hometown and began to teach his friends and family members; among the new believers he attracted were two black northerners who had come to Charleston to support striking hospital workers at the Medical University of South Carolina and had been among the hundreds jailed by local law enforcement. There seemed to be receptivity everywhere: in new and established localities, in rural and urban places, on college campuses and military bases, a trickle of new believers became a steady stream. Moses Richardson, an African American from Timmonsville, a small town near Florence, seemed to embody the more expansive approach to Bahá'í enrollment and membership called for by the House of Justice. Late in 1969, Richardson met some Bahá'ís by chance while walking home early one Sunday morning. He did not understand everything they told him, but he liked what he heard and it was cold out, so he quickly signed a membership card. Later, he contacted Jordan Young in Florence and began to associate with the local community. "I found myself getting more involved," Richardson recalled, "reading the literature, until finally I realized that I had believed these things, especially racial unity, most of my life. I must have been a Bahá'í all my life and claimed I was a Baptist." Richardson would eventually become one of the foremost teachers and administrators of the faith in the state.[59]

A new body, the State Goals Committee, formed when the previous Regional Teaching Committees were discontinued in 1966, coordinated statewide teaching efforts as well as public affairs. In March 1968, for example, only weeks after state law enforcement officers opened fire on black student demonstrators at State College in Orangeburg, a delegation of Columbia Bahá'ís presented Governor Robert McNair with a copy of *The Proclamation of Bahá'u'lláh*, a special volume prepared by the House of Justice for the centennial observance. After Martin Luther King's assassination in April, the State Goals Committee sent a

Participants in the South Carolina Bahá'í State Convention, Masonic Temple, Columbia, November 1968. The 1968 convention was three times as large as the one just two years earlier, with almost 50 adults voting in person and 20 children and youth also present. Around the state, the number of adult believers had nearly doubled to 132, and the faith's geographic base had broadened considerably. *Personal collection of Dorothy Frye.*

telegram of condolence to his widow on behalf of the South Carolina Bahá'í community. In the fall, the committee presented a statement by the National Spiritual Assembly about racism and the urban uprisings, titled "Why Our Cities Burn," to state officials. At the same time, the statewide community adopted a bold set of expansion goals. At the 1968 state convention, which was three times as large as the one just two years earlier, participants committed to forming three new Local Spiritual Assemblies per year in 1969, 1970, and 1971 and four per year in 1972 and 1973, for a total of nineteen in the state by the end of the Nine Year Plan. Compared to the painfully slow growth of the previous decades, the goals represented an audacious vision, no doubt spurred by the National Spiritual Assembly's letter to the state conventions expressing confidence "that large-scale conversion is not a far-distant goal." Little did they know, however, that their efforts would result in far more substantial growth than they had imagined.[60]

Quickening

In 1969, communications from the National Spiritual Assembly and its agencies took on an even greater tone of excitement and urgency, and in September, the National Teaching Committee hosted the Southern Teaching Conference in Chattanooga, Tennessee, in order to prepare a new regional plan. A letter to participants from the National Spiritual Assembly called for a "redoubled effort" to realize "large-scale expansion" in the South, with particular attention to the African American population. During the conference, the National Teaching Committee presented its newly-appointed subsidiary body, the Deep South Committee, that would spearhead the effort. The new committee announced goals for establishing the faith in new localities in each state; for South Carolina, the whopping total was twenty-four towns, most of them small county seats, by the end of the Nine Year Plan in a little more than two years.[61]

Participants returned to their homes from Chattanooga determined to bring about the anticipated surge in enrollments. By early 1970, believers around the country were reading in the *American Bahá'í*, a new monthly publication of the National Spiritual Assembly, that dozens of people had embraced the faith over a period of months in the small towns of Dawson, Georgia, and Bogalusa, Louisiana. From Adams Run, a rural hamlet thirty miles from downtown Charleston, came a startling headline: "19 Declarations in 36 Hours." Alberta Deas, a graduate of State College who had become a Bahá'í while living in Alabama, had returned to her family home of Adams Run after taking a job in Charleston. She reported that several people, including members of her family and other neighbors, including young people, had embraced the faith during a series of home visits and firesides. "[A]ll of a sudden," Deas wrote of one meeting, "as if there was a burst of fire in the room, the young people were asking for [enrollment] cards." Addressing the national community directly, Deas wrote: "[T]he people here are waiting for the Message of Bahá'u'lláh and are ready to accept it. I haven't had time to visit them, because of my job, the distance I have to travel, and late hours. However, everyone seems to think that the 'popcorn has just begun to pop.'"[62]

In March 1970, the Deep South Committee, hoping to build on these successes, hosted a second teaching conference at Penn Center just for the states of South Carolina, Georgia, Alabama, Mississippi, and Louisiana. Along with two members of the National Spiritual Assembly and other representatives of the national administration, the committee trained some three hundred Bahá'ís from the five focus states in the methods and materials for teaching rural people that had proven effective in other national communities, including the use of a "simple and direct teaching kit." The Deep South Committee identified fifteen goal localities, three in each state, in which to try the new approach and received commitments from sixty conference participants to settle in or travel to the selected towns. According to one report, "Some…made on-the-spot decisions to pioneer and left right after the conference to move to their chosen localities." Before they left, participants gathered for prayers at the grave of Abraham Brown, a member of St. Helena Island's first Local Spiritual Assembly who had died the year before. Brown had "spent the last years of his life clearing…property" to be used for a Bahá'í cemetery on the island and "insisted that he be buried there"—an important marker of his new religious identity in a culture where church burials held great significance. Glenford Mitchell, the secretary of the National Spiritual Assembly, praised the conference participants for their spirit of devotion and enthusiasm. They were "so ablaze with the love of God," he said, "so uninhibited, that I don't think we will have any trouble in bringing in numbers; we may have trouble in managing the statistics."[63] Events would soon bear out both parts of Mitchell's prediction.

Teaching activities accelerated across the region during the year. In June, participants in the Southeastern Bahá'í Summer School in Fort Valley, Georgia, spurred by Hand of the Cause of God Amatu'l-Bahá Rúhíyyih Khánum, the widow of Shoghi Effendi, spread out in pairs to "three tiny towns" nearby and "enrolled 235 new believers in a period covering less than 24 hours." In August, a weekend youth project in Winnsboro, South Carolina, resulted in some 80 new believers. The movement even caught the attention of a national wire service, which announced in a story posted from Raleigh that the Bahá'í Faith had "demonstrated startling success in attracting black people of the South."

By the fall, it seemed clear that the American Bahá'í community was entering an unprecedented period of growth. In September, Hand of the Cause of God Enoch Olinga visited South Carolina as part of an extensive tour of the Americas. Meeting with the Deep South Committee at Penn Center, Olinga urged them to pursue audacious plans, constantly working to open up new areas to the faith while consolidating new communities. He told the committee to be completely confident: "[N]ever limit the power of the Holy Spirit to assist you. Goals are made to be surpassed.… All the institutions and friends around the world will be praying for your success with your teaching plans." Emboldened by such encouragement

First Local Spiritual Assembly of St. Helena Island (initially called Frogmore after the name of the local post office), 1963. Pictured here are, from left to right (*front*): Gracie Reddicks, Viola Chaplain, Helen Michaels, and Edna Ford; (*back*) William Reddicks, Janie Johnson, Abraham Brown, Virginia Green, and James Johnson. *National Bahá'í Archives.*

and by experiences across the region during the previous year, the Deep South Committee planned a three-month regional teaching campaign timed to take advantage of the winter school holidays. The campaign would include specific projects in each of the sixteen southern states, with overall regional goals of enrolling 30,000 new believers, opening 500 new localities, and forming 250 new Local Spiritual Assemblies. The committee planed at least twenty seminars to train believers, new and veteran, as members

Left: Hand of the Cause of God Amatu'l-Bahá Rúhíyyih Khánum (née Mary Maxwell, 1910–2000), U.S.-born widow of Shoghi Effendi. Long a vocal proponent of reaching the African American and Native American populations, she helped train teams of teachers at the 1970 Southeast Bahá'í Summer School in Fort Valley, Georgia. *National Bahá'í Archives*.

Right: Hand of the Cause of God Enoch Olinga (1926–1979), a Ugandan whom Shoghi Effendi called the "Father of Victories" for his role in establishing the faith across Central and West Africa, during his visit to the United States, autumn 1970. "Goals are meant to be surpassed," he told the Deep South Committee. *From the* American Bahá'í.

Members of the Deep South Committee with teachers and new believers in Henderson, North Carolina, summer 1970. While carried out largely as the result of multiple local initiatives, large-scale growth of the Bahá'í Faith in the South received critical impetus, coordination, and support from the National Spiritual Assembly and its agencies. *Personal collection of Fereydoun Jalali*.

of expansion and consolidation teams and teachers of Bahá'í classes for children. Following a briefing about the campaign in Montgomery, Alabama, in October, members of the region's State Goals Committees returned home to make preparations.[64]

THE DILLON CAMPAIGN

In South Carolina, three Bahá'í families in the Pee Dee region—Lee and Genelle Grimsley of Lake City, Roger and Sandy Roff of Dillon, and Jordan and Annette Young of Florence—agreed to coordinate and finance a two-week teaching project as part of the regional campaign. The project would be based in Dillon, a small county seat only five miles from the North Carolina border, and target all the towns in a thirty-mile radius. The area included the small cities of Florence, South Carolina, and Lumberton, North Carolina, but was otherwise a region of small towns and farms inhabited by almost equal numbers of blacks and whites. There also was a substantial Native American population, with the Pee Dees in Dillon and Marlboro Counties in South Carolina and the much more numerous Lumbees in Robeson and neighboring counties in North Carolina. Dillon was the practical choice for the project's headquarters because the Roffs were able to provide housing for the volunteer teachers at their house on Main Street and at a vacant rental property they owned a block away. They also rented a nearby lodge hall, the Woodmen of the World building, as a site for planning, meal preparation, and evening meetings. During most of the project, they were joined by Charles and Helen Thomas, who had only recently moved from nearby Laurinburg, North Carolina, to Rock Hill, and Poova Murday, a member of the Deep South Committee originally from Mauritius, as organizers. Bahá'ís from around South Carolina and visitors from other states—many of them young people and relatively new believers themselves—came for as much time as they could to work in the project.[65]

Each morning, participants "gathered for briefings, prayers, songs, [and] fellowship," after which teams fanned out to their assigned towns. Using simple, hand-colored teaching books and the "*Ebony* reprint," a large, full-color booklet based on an article on the faith from the popular African American magazine, they talked with people wherever they were, "[i]n laundromats, restaurants, night-clubs, on the streets, in yards, in the rain, in the mud, in the snow." Often the teachers attracted attention by

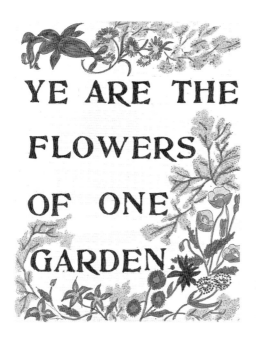

Passage from the writings of Bahá'u'lláh from a South Carolina teaching book, early 1970s. Participants were trained to use a simple, direct presentation of the history, teachings, laws, and practices of the Bahá'í Faith and decorated their own teaching books. *Personal collection of Annette Young.*

singing Bahá'í songs. Moses Richardson, then a relatively new believer from Florence, recalled of the project:

> *It was really cold sometimes, but we kept going. The more I went, the better I felt. The method we used was to tell everyone about Bahá'u'lláh and the Bahá'í Faith. I went to Dillon at least once or twice a week, and I would have gone more, except I was working. People were eager to learn....In Dillon we went to teach everyone, not discriminating between rich and poor, black or white....I heard about people having dreamed about 'Abdu'l-Bahá and expecting Bahá'ís to visit them.*

Sometimes, people who had just accepted the faith accompanied the teams to meet and teach their neighbors. In the evenings, the teachers held mass meetings for new Bahá'ís and their friends and family members in rented halls or large tents. Using inspirational speeches, singing, and short films, they made more in-depth presentations about Bahá'í history, teachings, and community, encouraging active participation from the audience. According to one account:

> *During the night almost all of the 80 people there became Bahá'ís and those who'd already declared experienced their first deepening class....*

BAHÁ'Í:
A way of life for millions

Lofty dome of America Bahá'í House of Worship, viewed from interior, reflects spirituality of faith. Disc in center of dome is holy symbol in the Bahá'í religion.

House of Worship in Wilmette, Illinois, is center of American Bahá'í community. Like great cathedrals of Europe, temple was built slowly and intermittently over a period of 50 years. The Bahá'í temple, which has been called a "Taj Mahal" of the West, is visited annually by thousands of tourists of all faiths. Wilmette is suburb of Chicago.

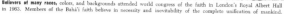

Believers of many races, colors, and backgrounds attended world congress of the faith in London's Royal Albert Hall in 1963. Members of the Bahá'í faith believe in necessity and inevitability of the complete unification of mankind.

At Bahá'í Institute, Green Lake, Wisconsin, Gina Browder, Danny Reimer stroll through woods.

The *"Ebony* reprint," early 1970s. Originally published in April 1965 under a cover story on the death of Nat King Cole, the lengthy article had already brought the Bahá'í Faith to the attention of many African Americans around the United States. Reprinted as a full-color booklet, it was used during teaching campaigns in the Deep South as a comprehensive introduction to the religion. *Author's personal collection.*

[S]ome of the audience joined us up front. Some of them sang for us, and
we parted only after all forming a big unity circle and sharing prayers for
unity and thanksgiving.

After the evening meetings, the teachers, exhausted and exhilarated, returned
to Dillon to debrief and sleep and prepare for another day.[66]
    While thousands identified themselves with the Bahá'í Faith during the
campaign, not everyone in the area was welcoming. One team, for example,
reported visiting the home of a new believer for the first Nineteen Day Feast in
that town and finding "a woman preacher there with some youth supporters.
She had come because she felt it was her duty to tell them that they were losing
their salvation by forgetting about Jesus." The teachers diffused the situation
by reversing the normal order of the meeting and having refreshments first,
after which the minister left. Some opposition was more vicious. Local police
chased teaching teams out of Bishopville, the seat of Lee County, two days in
a row before some of the Bahá'ís met with the police chief, explained the faith
to him, and received his assurance that they would no longer be bothered.
In Dillon, the houses where teachers slept were repeatedly threatened with
circling cars and a bomb threat. Sandy Roff recalled:

> *The Ku Klux Klan stepped in and warned us. Our kids were threatened,*
> *and we were told if they should go to school, we would never see them*
> *again. Roger's life was threatened, and his patients would not come. Our*
> *business went down, and our bills piled up. People who had extended credit*
> *before now demanded repayment. One day I was walking uptown, and a*
> *man spit in my face and called me a dirty n----r-loving SOB....It took all*
> *I had to say "I love you" and keep from crying.[67]*

As they had since early in the century, however, the Bahá'ís took
opposition from racial and religious conservatives as a sign of success. The
faith's national and international institutions hailed the unprecedented
results of the Dillon campaign and encouraged its participants to persevere.
Even before the project ended, the front page of the January 1971 issue of
the *American Bahá'í* announced the national movement's "greatest teaching
victory" ever, some six thousand new believers in the Carolinas achieved
"within two weeks." Later the same month, the Universal House of Justice
shared with the worldwide community via telegram the news of "entry by
troops," a stage of rapid growth predicted in the faith's scriptures, in South
Carolina, including the latest tally of new believers:

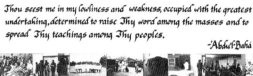

FEBRUARY 1971

The American Bahá'í

Published by the National Teaching Committee for the National Spiritual Assembly of the Bahá'ís of the United States

South Responds To Divine Summons

Over 8000 Souls Respond to the Healing Message of Bahá'u'lláh in the Carolinas, Hundreds More in Arkansas, Kentucky, Mississippi, Oklahoma and Tennessee

The opening sentence of the prayer for the Southern states describes the activities of the devoted followers of Bahá'u'lláh in the South. Like a strong but gentle wind, the Army of Bahá'u'lláh is fanning the flame of faith in the hearts of the masses. One by one, all of the southern states are experiencing within their borders the large-scale enrollment of peoples into the Faith of the Lord of Hosts. Alabama, Georgia, Florida, Louisiana, Texas, Virginia and West Virginia have already witnessed the beginning of this cherished wish of 'Abdu'l-Bahá and this oft-expressed hope of Shoghi Effendi.

Guided by the instructions of our infallible Universal House of Justice and the continuous supervision of our National Spiritual Assembly, mass teaching is developing more and more effective ways to handle the challenges which such an influx of new believers poses. Mass teaching means mass proclamation, mass expansion and mass consolidation. It means that the three prerequisites for successful teaching enumerated by the beloved Guardian in The Advent of Divine Justice must be strictly adhered to (i.e. rectitude of conduct, chaste and holy life, and freedom from racial prejudice). The Bahá'í standard cannot be compromised. It must be held high like a beacon light. Mass teaching requires it, and continued success in this vital work demands it. The following articles and pictures capture but a small part of the excitement, dedication and love of God that our brothers and sisters in the mass teaching fields everywhere are reflecting.

The dramatic first issue of the national Bahá'í newspaper following the southern regional teaching campaign of winter 1970–71. The influx of thousands of new believers, most of them African Americans from small towns and rural hamlets, permanently changed the identity, structures, and expectations of the Bahá'í movement in the United States. *From the American Bahá'í.*

Joyfully announce…process entry by troops accelerating United States evidenced by enrollment eight thousand new believers South Carolina course six weeks campaign raising number new believers entire country 13000 since Ridván. Process gathering momentum. Indications similar development occurring new areas North South America. May valiant workers Faith toiling throughout world gain confidence added strength these uplifting victories won in His name reap similar harvest homefronts all continents.

By the spring, the National Spiritual Assembly could report that all the domestic expansion goals of the Nine Year Plan had not only been met but also exceeded, two years ahead of schedule. Bahá'í membership in the United States had more than doubled in a single administrative year, "with most of the new adherents, some 20,000, residing in the Deep South alone."[68]

A "Completely New Phase"

As thrilling as the surge in enrollments during late 1970 and early 1971 was, the National Assembly admitted that it would "tax to the utmost" the community's means for "absorbing huge numbers of new believers and ensuring the transformation of their lives in conformity with Bahá'í principles." Indeed, growth in South Carolina and elsewhere overwhelmed the capacity of the national administration even to keep track. In a single day during the Dillon campaign, for example, over one thousand people signed enrollment cards, swamping the part-time membership clerk at the national office in Wilmette. In addition to augmenting the national staff, the National Assembly anticipated that growth would require strengthening Local Spiritual Assemblies, revamping the system of State Conventions to take into account a much larger electorate, and experimenting with new methods of communication and education for much larger numbers of children, youth, and adults than ever before. The "administration of the Cause in the United States," the National Assembly asserted, was "entering a completely new phase."[69]

Meanwhile, on the ground in South Carolina, participants in the Dillon campaign were already coming to terms with some of the challenges resulting from the surge of growth. For one thing, the intense activity of the winter project had taken a toll on the core organizers. As Roger Roff recalled: "I had to put my finances back together, try and get my practice going [again], maintain my family and my home." Likewise, most of the out-of-state teachers returned home to their schools and jobs after a few weeks. While smaller contingents of local Bahá'ís continued the campaign on weekends, making return visits to recently established communities and opening up new localities, as Roff put it, "There just weren't enough people to continue teaching and consolidating." For those who did stay involved, the relative remoteness of many of the new believers and the acute poverty and limited literacy that many of them faced made for serious logistical challenges. As one observer noted:

> The problems of relocating rural people were very real....Many of the people who had become Bahá'ís were illiterate, and their card had to be written out for them. Many of the cards were illegible. People had given their post office box number or general delivery as an address, and there is virtually no way to find a person using this information. They live on country roads which are not accurately mapped, several families using one post box which was located in town at the post office.

By the spring of 1971, the national office had processed the enrollments of some 5,700 voting-age Bahá'ís in South Carolina, up from 624 the previous year. The State Goals Committee organized teams to assist with the establishment of scores of new Local Spiritual Assemblies at Ridván. Whereas the previous year there had been 8 such bodies in the state, 108 were formed in 1971—rivaling only California for the most Local Assemblies in the country.[70]

As impressive as this accomplishment was, simply holding elections for Local Assemblies was hardly enough to ensure their proper functioning or, more broadly, to ensure that patterns of Bahá'í individual and collective life took root in dozens of localities across the state. Further growth in South Carolina—or, indeed, simply maintaining the community at its new, larger size—would depend on mobilizing many more believers within the state, both new and veteran, as teachers and organizers. Indeed, the surge of growth during the southern campaign prompted the National Spiritual Assembly to make a number of changes designed to involve more of the grassroots of the community in the planning and implementation of teaching activities. Shortly after Ridván, it announced that the country's State Goals Committees would be replaced by some eighty District Teaching Committees, with fifteen states initially subdivided into smaller areas. South Carolina would have four District Teaching Committees responsible for approximately the northwestern, north-central, eastern, and southern portions of the state, respectively. Within a few months, the eastern district, which included the counties of the Pee Dee and counted the largest number of believers, was further divided for a total of five. In addition, as the state with by far the largest Bahá'í population in the country, South Carolina would have its own Regional Teaching Committee on a par with four others that would serve the rest of the southern and the northeastern, central, and western states. Initially composed of Alberta Deas, Sandy Roff, and Elting Smalls of St. Helena Island—all South Carolina natives who had been instrumental in the mass teaching work—the Regional Teaching Committee quickly opened an office in suburban Charleston, with Deas serving as committee secretary and full-time office manager. The regional and district committees were given enormous responsibilities: to plan and execute teaching projects and open new localities, to foster the establishment and development of Local Spiritual Assemblies, to coordinate the services of traveling teachers and recruit and settle pioneers, to enroll new believers in areas not served by a Local Assembly, and to maintain accurate membership lists for their respective territories.[71]

Dormitory of the Louis G. Gregory Bahá'í Institute under construction near Hemingway, 1971. The permanent facility was one of the first "teaching institutes" in the world, called for by the Universal House of Justice to be established in regions of large-scale growth. *National Bahá'í Archives.*

As the new committee structure was being established, some of the leaders of the Dillon campaign asked the National Assembly to establish a permanent "teaching institute"—an agency that the Universal House of Justice had called for in areas of large-scale growth to train new teachers and administrators of the faith—and a radio station to help consolidate new believers in isolated rural areas. As valuable as summer and winter schools and other occasional trainings and seminars had been for many years, it was already clear that they would hardly be able to meet the educational needs of a much larger community. While the question of the radio station was deferred, the National Assembly agreed on the need for a permanent training facility that could be open year-round. Jordan and Annette Young knew of a property that seemed appropriate. Paul and Merie Douglas, pastors of an independent church on a 130-acre portion of wooded family land in Georgetown County near Hemingway, were patients of theirs who had recently become Bahá'ís. The Douglases' conversion had split the congregation, with some following them into the Bahá'í community and others not, leaving an unfinished church building, substantial debt, and, in a religion with no clergy, two former pastors with no livelihood. At the Youngs' urging, the National Assembly purchased the property, satisfying the Douglases' debt, and began construction of facilities for a teaching institute.[72]

The Army of Light and the Shape of Consolidation

By late 1971 and early 1972, the national rate of enrollments had dropped considerably, and the faith's senior institutions attempted to rally the community both to continue growth in the Deep South and replicate the breakthrough that had occurred there in other parts of the country. Contributing to the sense of urgency was Hand of the Cause of God Rúhíyyih Khánum. "Do keep up the momentum," she counseled in one letter published in the *American Bahá'í*, "for such waves are not steady but have to ridden right in to the shore. I think all over the world there are opportunities right now that are priceless and unique…so now is the time to run ahead like a grass fire and let nothing stop us but some major change over which we have no control, and not our own folly or a fit of cautiousness." Jane Faily McCants, an Atlanta physician who served South Carolina as Auxiliary Board member (one of the deputies of the Hands of the Cause tasked with supporting expansion and consolidation at the regional level), wrote that some two hundred new pioneers were needed to assure the consolidation of the state's new local communities. "Without them," she warned, "a promise is broken, a trust betrayed. The black people of the South who accepted Bahá'u'lláh will be left with words, not deeds." In a February 1972 letter to the National Spiritual Assembly, the Universal House of Justice struck a similar note, calling the national community not only to fully support the expansion and consolidation work in the South but to adopt everywhere the approaches that had met with such success in South Carolina. "Far from standing aloof," the House of Justice wrote, "the American believers are called upon now, as never before, to grasp this golden opportunity which has been presented to them, to consult together prayerfully and widen the scope of their endeavors." While sparing no effort in the South, the House of Justice said that "[e]fforts to reach the minorities should be increased and broadened to include…the Indians, Spanish-speaking people, Japanese and Chinese." The key going forward would be for the entire national community to act "with the spirit which is conquering the citadels of the southern states."[73]

In January 1972, a renewed campaign of expansion and consolidation in South Carolina, planned with the assistance of Hand of the Cause of God Rahmátu'lláh Muhájir, was launched at a conference in Charleston. Meeting at the historic Francis Marion Hotel, some five hundred believers from South Carolina and other states learned about the specific plans of each District Teaching Committee and volunteered their support. The two-pronged effort would include consolidating the gains made since the beginning of the Dillon project and bringing "even larger-scale growth" to all parts of the state, with goals of increasing the number of Local Spiritual Assemblies, opening new localities to the faith, training new believers, involving children in all the community's activities, and "strengthen[ing] the social fabric and quality of Bahá'í life." Muhájir brought two experienced coordinators, both Auxiliary Board members serving other regions, to South Carolina for the effort. Jenabe Caldwell had recently spearheaded a successful campaign, dubbed the "Army of Light," to bring the faith to virtually all of the far-flung towns and villages of Alaska, and Thelma Thomas had helped spur large-scale growth in Louisiana. Together, they led a new Army of Light consisting of twenty or so full-time teachers, mostly youth in their teens and twenties. Beginning in North Augusta, where the state's first Bahá'í settler had taken up residence more than sixty years before, the project moved generally eastward across the state employing methods similar to those used in the Dillon campaign, with teaching in teams during the day and mass meetings in the evening. This time, however, "pre-teams" visited each locality first in order to find accommodations for the volunteers and venues for the evening meetings, to secure permission from local authorities to work in the town, and to seek publicity from the media. According to one account, it "often took days" to find a meeting place for interracial groups. Consolidation teams, whether in new localities or those that had been affected by the Dillon campaign, focused on visiting the homes of new believers, often giving them Bahá'í prayer books and studying deepening booklets prepared by the National Teaching Committee. They also helped prepare new Bahá'ís for the election of Local Spiritual Assemblies, in many areas for the first time. However, only 69 Local Spiritual Assemblies were elected at Ridván 1972, down from 108 in the immediate aftermath of the Dillon project the previous year. Even with the deployment of full-time teachers, the logistical challenges of consolidation remained formidable.[74]

As the statewide teaching project wound down during the summer of 1972, the District Teaching Committees—now numbering six with the division of the southern portion of the state into two districts—and the handful of

Hand of the Cause of God Rahmatu'lláh Muhájir (1923–1979), Louis Gregory Institute, 1970s. An Iranian physician and pioneer to Indonesia during the Ten Year Plan, Muhájir was an early and ardent advocate of teaching rural people around the world. *Louis G. Gregory Bahá'í Institute.*

strong Local Spiritual Assemblies remained the principal means for consolidating new believers and communities. With a focus on local planning and execution, veteran South Carolina Bahá'ís, newly arrived pioneers, and a growing number of new believers worked in concert to build the institutions and practices of Bahá'í community life in cities and towns across the state. The District Teaching Committees focused a great deal of attention on establishing and strengthening Local Spiritual Assemblies, a task made somewhat easier in the final year of the Nine Year Plan when the Universal House of Justice allowed a new or lapsed Local Assembly to be formed anytime during the year instead of waiting for the first day of Ridván 1973. The National Spiritual Assembly developed materials for a one-day training program prior to the election and new manuals for local secretaries and treasurers. But their efforts were felt more broadly, strengthening even the established communities. In Greenville, for example, where some three hundred people had become Bahá'ís during the Army of Light campaign, there was a full slate of activities, including firesides and multiple classes for children and adults, held in a number of homes throughout the city. With some twenty local communities under its purview, the District Teaching Committee serving Greenville divided its territory into four sectors, each with its own consolidation team. Other District Teaching Committees experimented with similar methods. For example, in District 5, serving part of the Pee Dee, the committee assembled two groups of "workers," one to coordinate the movement of traveling teachers in the area and the other consisting of five consolidation teams focused on Local Spiritual Assembly training. The workers gathered regularly for planning and reflection.[75]

By the end of 1972, barely two years since the beginning of the Dillon campaign, the effects of the breakthrough in teaching were apparent across the state, with weekly firesides, deepening classes, or children's classes in more than twenty-five places, including hamlets of only a few hundred people such as Richburg (Chester County), Starr (Anderson County), and Van Wyck (Lancaster County). While many of the new Bahá'í communities in rural areas depended on the presence of homefront pioneers or visitors from nearby established communities, a few flourished with minimal outside assistance. One example was Aynor, a town of fewer than six hundred people in rural Horry County. There, Wilbur and Ilena Vereen, whose relatives had first heard of the faith as patients of Jordan and Annette Young, became Bahá'ís in April 1971 and quickly became the motors of an energetic new Bahá'í community with regular children's classes, a Local Spiritual Assembly that needed minimal outside assistance, and their own teaching projects to reach all the residents of Aynor and two adjacent hamlets. In October 1972, when more than two hundred Bahá'ís and friends from around South Carolina gathered for a social event at Santee State Park, sixty-two of them came from Aynor, the largest group from a single local community.[76]

The gathering at Santee State Park was one of a number of occasions, formal and informal, that helped "strengthen the social fabric and quality of Bahá'í life" for a statewide community that was spread across many localities and included so many people who were new to the faith. Even such longstanding events as summer and winter schools gained a new lease on life with more participants, especially young people. In August 1972, for example, Hand of the Cause of God William Sears was the main speaker at the Carolinas Bahá'í Summer School, held at Kings Mountain State Park near Blacksburg. After the school, one report noted that nine youth from Oakridge, an unincorporated hamlet in nearby York County, had returned home "bubbling with enthusiasm." The following week, "when the pioneers for that area arrived [in Oakridge] for the regular meeting, they discovered that the school had inspired the young Bahá'ís to begin teaching. Seven of their friends became Bahá'ís that evening." The community quickly grew to more than thirty people, most of them teenagers.[77]

Hand of the Cause of God William Sears (1911–1992) wearing a necktie with the image of the South Carolina state flag, date unknown. A Minnesota native who left a career in broadcasting to promote the Bahá'í Faith in Africa, Sears traveled widely as a Hand of the Cause and took a special interest in expansion and consolidation in South Carolina. *Personal collection of Mark Perry.*

THE LOUIS G. GREGORY BAHÁ'Í INSTITUTE

In October 1972, hundreds of people from across South Carolina and visitors from around the country gathered for a weekend of activities to dedicate the Louis G. Gregory Bahá'í Institute. More than six decades after the state's native son had alerted a small, overwhelmingly white, mostly northern community to the extraordinary receptivity of black southerners to the faith's message, a very different national movement was opening its first permanent agency dedicated to training new believers, most of them African Americans, as teachers and administrators. Appropriately, the new campus was almost equidistant between Gregory's ancestral plantation near Florence and his birthplace in Charleston. The Continental Board of Counselors—an institution created by the Universal House of Justice in 1968 to carry into the future the functions of the Hands of the Cause—organized a two-day Deepening Conference at the Myrtle Beach Convention Center prior to the dedication ceremony. Several of the speakers explained their personal connections to Louis Gregory, and references to him as a teacher of the faith, as an architect of its national administrative structure, and as an activist for interracial unity ran throughout the sessions.

On Sunday, October 22, some one thousand people gathered on the grounds of the newly completed Institute for the dedication. Set amid farmland and pine forests outside of Hemingway, the facility consisted of a cluster of modest structures—including a classroom and office building, a forty-bed dormitory, and a caretaker's cottage. The program consisted of devotional readings, brief talks, and musical selections. In his remarks, Harold Jackson, the newly appointed dean of the Institute, called it a "gift to the people of the South." Hand of the Cause of God William Sears, unable to attend in person, recorded an audio message for the gathering, calling Louis Gregory a "great American hero." Finally, Firuz Kazemzadeh, chairman of the National Spiritual Assembly, declared the Institute open. Afterward, the attendees stayed for musical entertainment, tours of the buildings, and fellowship on the grounds.[78]

Shortly after the conference and dedication ceremony for the Institute in October 1972, the National Spiritual Assembly appointed a council to oversee its functions. With a mandate to "set the standard for Bahá'í learning," the dean and council began to plan programs and assemble a roster of volunteer faculty. Teachers were drawn from experienced believers in the state and region, while a task force of education professors and graduate students appointed by the National Teaching Committee

Deepening Conference prior to the dedication of the Louis G. Gregory Bahá'í Institute, Myrtle Beach Convention Center, October 1972. *National Bahá'í Archives.*

Young participants in the Deepening Conference. *National Bahá'í Archives.*

Dr. Sarah Martin Pereira (1909–1995), member of the National Spiritual Assembly, addressing participants at the dedication program of the Louis G. Gregory Bahá'í Institute, October 1972. Pereira noted that her family had become Bahá'ís during a 1913 visit to Cleveland by Louis Gregory. *National Bahá'í Archives.*

A new Bahá'í from Saluda at the dedication of the Louis Gregory Institute. Friends and family members had warned him not to travel across the state in a car with whites, but he came anyway. *National Bahá'í Archives.*

Participants in the dedication of the Louis Gregory Institute exploring the campus after the program. The Institute's facilities initially consisted of a classroom building and a dormitory. *National Bahá'í Archives*.

focused on developing curricula. The first classes, on the topic of the "World Order of Bahá'u'lláh," took place in late December 1972 and were taught by Auxiliary Board members Jane McCants and Thelma Thomas (now Khelghati after her recent marriage), who had helped coordinate the Army of Light project. At the end of January 1973, Hand of the Cause of God William Sears and Firuz Kazemzadeh, who was a professor of history at Yale University, taught another weekend program. In February, March, and April, the focus was on "training field workers to help form Local Spiritual Assemblies and get them functioning during the closing days of the Nine Year Plan." In May, the Institute introduced a five-day course designed primarily to deepen new believers, which it planned to repeat several times and evaluate. During the summer, there were weeklong programs for youth of different age groups. Weekend programs during the year included classes on the Covenant and on a newly released synopsis and codification of the Kitáb-i-Aqdas ("Most Holy Book"), Bahá'u'lláh's book of laws.[79]

The opening of the Louis Gregory Institute marked the end of a brief period that had dramatically changed the face of the Bahá'í Faith in the

United States. At the time of the first southern teaching conference in Chattanooga in 1969, there were about two hundred believers in a handful of localities in South Carolina, but by the end of the Nine Year Plan in early 1973, there were upward of fifteen thousand. Almost overnight, the South Carolina community had gone from a small, scattered network to a budding mass movement with members in every county of the state, and within the American Bahá'í community as a whole, South Carolina had become a giant, accounting for approximately a quarter of all the believers in the country. Not only had the national community's geographic center shifted dramatically, but its cultural identity and aspirations were changing as well. By means of firsthand testimonials shared by those who had served as traveling teachers in the southern campaign; the stories, photographs, and notices from South Carolina and other Deep South states that now claimed a great deal of space in national Bahá'í publications; and the written and verbal endorsements of the faith's national and global leaders, mass teaching in South Carolina came to define a new set of expectations and a new collective identity—one that was blacker, more southern, and more rural—for the Bahá'í Faith in the United States. The surge of growth led some to predict that South Carolina would eventually become "the first all-Bahá'í state in the country." Whether or not that was to be the case, the road ahead would be infinitely more complex and difficult than anyone at the Chattanooga conference had imagined. Indeed, the swelling membership in South Carolina and elsewhere would severely test the capacity of the national administration to maintain unity of vision in an increasingly diverse community and to marshal the necessary resources, human and financial, to support continued growth. This tension—between high expectations on the one hand and practical challenges on the other—would define the next several decades in South Carolina and in the national Bahá'í movement as a whole.[80]

"Hand in Hand"

The Era of Experimentation, 1973–1996

During the quarter century after the southern teaching campaign of 1970–71, South Carolina would remain at the center of the American Bahá'í movement's efforts to learn how to sustain large-scale growth, introduce it in other parts of the country, and successfully integrate new believers into an increasingly dynamic Bahá'í community life that could contribute to social progress. Institutions and individuals in South Carolina, including successive generations of new believers, engaged in intense, sustained, and creative activity along a number of related fronts, experimenting with a variety of approaches to teaching, training, and community development. While a new large burst of enrollments failed to materialize, growth continued in more modest—and probably more manageable—fashion during the rest of the 1970s, largely initiated at the local level. Through individual teaching initiatives, the deployment of pioneers and traveling teachers, and periodic collective campaigns, the size and geographic scope of the movement continued to grow; by the end of the decade, there were Bahá'ís in some 440 towns and hamlets in South Carolina, with more than 180 Local Spiritual Assemblies and regular firesides and classes for children and adults in many localities. At the same time, sustained attention to the objectives of successive global plans, particularly the focus on Local Spiritual Assemblies, yielded a great deal more knowledge and experience about consolidation and the development of local Bahá'í community life. The overarching goal of mobilizing thousands of believers as confident protagonists in the faith's development remained elusive, but by the end of the 1970s, the number of such workers across the state reached the hundreds, and a variety of efforts intended to ensure that there would be even more in the next generation were in place. Moreover, during the decade, a number of elements—for example, a high degree of racial and sexual equality; extensive use of the arts, particularly singing, in all phases of community life; widespread participation by children and youth; a pronounced rurality; the centrality of the Louis Gregory Institute; attention to community history and to learning about the processes of growth; a tradition of effective statewide planning, coordination, and collaboration among institutions; and the persistence of large-scale growth as an overriding goal and expectation—emerged and coalesced into a South Carolina Bahá'í culture that was both vibrant and distinctive.[81]

A new burst of rapid growth, accompanied by the establishment of the American community's first radio station on the campus of the Louis Gregory Institute, took place in the mid-1980s. Overall, however, during the 1980s and 1990s, the mood of the national Bahá'í movement was one of disenchantment with large-scale growth. The national community increasingly devoted its human and financial resources to other matters, including developing Sunday schools for Bahá'í children in metropolitan areas, integrating thousands of Iranian Bahá'í refugees fleeing the 1979 Islamic Revolution, and using the mass media to broadcast the faith's teachings. All were areas to which the Universal House of Justice had called the community's attention; nevertheless, the shift in focus of the national movement, combined with ongoing rural population loss in South Carolina, resulted in a general decline in teaching activities and Bahá'í community life in many localities. The situation in South Carolina, as in other parts of the world that had been struggling with the implications of large-scale growth, prompted the Universal House of Justice to devise a fresh series of global plans beginning in the late 1990s.[82]

THE INTERIM YEAR AND THE FIVE YEAR PLAN (1973–1979)

In January 1973, the Universal House of Justice announced that the next global teaching plan would not be launched until Ridván 1974, leaving an interim year during which National Spiritual Assemblies were directed to pursue their own plans, including those for "developing and enriching Bahá'í community life" and "fostering youth activity." The last months of the

Nine Year Plan and the interim year also included key developments at the Bahá'í World Center that would have long-term effects in South Carolina. In June 1972, the Universal House of Justice announced that the increased workload at the World Center had made it necessary to begin construction of its new permanent seat—the second in the complex of administrative buildings that Shoghi Effendi had anticipated along a broad arc-shaped path adjacent to the Shrine of the Báb. In mid-1973, it announced the creation of the International Teaching Center, composed initially of three members appointed as Counselors and all of the living Hands of the Cause, which would assume supervision of the Continental Boards of Counselors and their auxiliaries and design and manage future global teaching plans. A few months later, the House of Justice increased the number of Auxiliary Board members around the world and authorized them to appoint assistants to help stimulate local community life and the development of Local Spiritual Assemblies.[83]

With the faith's administrative structure significantly augmented—from the grassroots to the World Center—the Universal House of Justice introduced a Five Year Plan (1974–79) with three broad objectives: "consolidation of the victories won" during the previous decade, a "vast and widespread expansion of the Bahá'í community," and "development of the distinctive character of Bahá'í life," particularly at the local level. Reflecting new needs for a faith that had seen the initial success of mass teaching in many countries, the House of Justice called national communities everywhere to give specific attention to the welfare of children and youth and to the development of Local Spiritual Assemblies. The education and nurturing of children and youth, it wrote, was an "essential obligation" both of parents and communities that must become a "firmly established Bahá'í activity." As for the strengthening of Local Assemblies, the "basic administrative unit" of the faith operating "at the first levels of human society," the House of Justice stated that success in this one area would "greatly enrich the quality of Bahá'í life" and better equip the faith to deal with large-scale growth. This dual emphasis directly influenced the activities of South Carolina's Bahá'ís during the Five Year Plan and remained prominent in the community's culture and identity for decades.[84]

South Carolina also figured prominently in the American Bahá'í community's domestic goals for the Five Year Plan, albeit indirectly. Echoing the themes it had outlined in its February 14, 1972 letter to the National Spiritual Assembly about extending the southern teaching program across the country, the Universal House of Justice assigned a set of domestic goals that took into account the national community's new reality: increasing

Members of the Local Spiritual Assembly of Newberry, 1974. *From left to right*: Emma Lee Hill (secretary), Edward Alston (chair), Lois Jones (treasurer), and Frankie Jones. The establishment and development of large numbers of Local Assemblies was a major focus of Bahá'í teaching plans in South Carolina during the 1970s and 1980s. *National Bahá'í Archives.*

the number of Local Assemblies to 1,400, including at least 25 on Indian reservations; expanding the use of radio and television, both for proclaiming the faith to a larger portion of the population and for "deepening the faith of the believers, particularly in rural areas"; and initiating teaching campaigns not only among the indigenous, Latino, Chinese, and Japanese populations but also among such European immigrant communities as the Armenians, Basques, and Greeks. The House of Justice also called for "intensive teaching and consolidation plans" to begin the process of entry by troops in at least three of the states that 'Abdu'l-Bahá had visited in 1912—none of which, owing to the paucity of Bahá'ís there at the time, had been in the Deep South. In the next few months, the National Spiritual Assembly chose New York, Illinois, and California for this purpose. Clearly, the House of Justice intended for mass teaching not to be confined to the South or to African Americans. During the course of the plan, the National Assembly and its agencies, along with the Hands of the Cause, the Counselors, and their auxiliaries, expended a great deal of energy to rally the entire national community to the ambitious domestic teaching goals. However, despite small successes in a number of areas, it seemed impossible to achieve a breakthrough in large-scale growth outside the Deep South.[85]

Administrative Arrangements

In preparation for the Five Year Plan, the National Spiritual Assembly decided to reduce costs and administrative duplication by eliminating the Regional Teaching Committees around the country—except for the one serving the single state of South Carolina, which was instead augmented with additional members. In late 1974, when Alberta Deas left for Massachusetts to pursue a doctorate in education, she was replaced as secretary by Trudy White, an African American who had recently moved to the Charleston area from Los Angeles. Near the beginning of the plan, the number of District Teaching Committees was increased to eight, enabling dozens of people in South Carolina—new and veteran believers, longtime residents and pioneers—to gain valuable experience in Bahá'í administration and become intimately familiar with communities beyond their own locality. In addition to the formidable tasks associated with establishing and nurturing new Local Spiritual Assemblies, the District Teaching Committees sponsored a variety of expansion and consolidation activities, for example, deploying visiting teachers; training believers in the use of new materials; helping to start children's classes and youth clubs in high schools and colleges; hosting picnics, dances, and other opportunities for fellowship; and organizing teaching projects in specific localities over weekends or longer periods.[86]

In addition to being an arena for the organization of teaching, the districts also served as electoral units for the selection of delegates to the National Convention, and the District Teaching Committees planned and conducted annual district conventions that took the place of the previous state convention. With the distribution of the 171 delegates roughly proportional to Bahá'í population, most districts around the country elected only 1, but in South Carolina there were so many Bahá'ís that six of the eight districts elected 3, 4, 5, or 6 delegates. Usually daylong affairs held in rented facilities, district conventions became important annual venues not only for community consultation but also for social bonding and identity formation; most included children's programs, singing, and communal meals. South Carolina's large number of delegates made an impression at the national level. In 1974, for example, 27 of the 29 delegates allotted to South Carolina were able to attend the National Convention, the largest group ever to attend from a single state. With no caucusing, nominations, or exit polling permitted in Bahá'í elections, it is impossible to say that the large number of delegates from South Carolina had any direct bearing on

Trudy White (1924–2009, *left*) and Alberta Deas (1934–2016, *right*) with an unidentified Bahá'í (*center*), Louis Gregory Institute, early 1970s. Deas was the first secretary of the South Carolina Regional Teaching Committee (1971–74) and later served as administrator of the Louis Gregory Institute and member of the National Spiritual Assembly. White served as a member, secretary, and field coordinator of the Regional Teaching Committee (1974–86) and Auxiliary Board member (1986–96). *Louis G. Gregory Bahá'í Institute.*

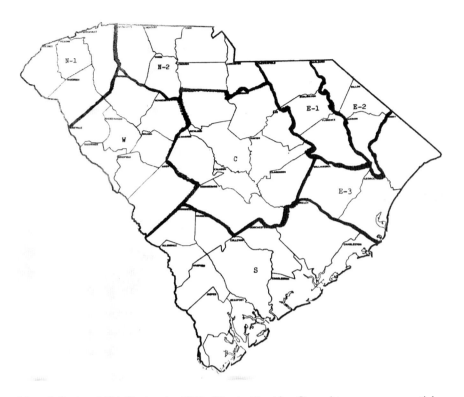

Map of districts, 1974. During the 1970s, District Teaching Committees were an essential element of Bahá'í administration in South Carolina. Districts also served as electoral units for selection of delegates to the Bahá'í National Convention. *From the* South Carolina Regional Bahá'í Bulletin.

the membership of the National Spiritual Assembly. However, individuals with extensive experience in large-scale growth in the South did serve on that body: Magdalene Carney, a young black Mississippian who had been a member of the Deep South Committee, was elected every year from 1970 to 1982, and Alberta Deas was elected every year from 1983 to 1997. Others elected from South Carolina were Jack McCants of Greenwood (1986 to 2001), a white man originally from Texas and a strong advocate of Bahá'í interracial activities since the 1950s, and Tod Ewing of Columbia (1992 to 1994), an African American pioneer originally from Minnesota.[87]

While the national and local Spiritual Assemblies and the teaching committee structure were prominent in the organization of the community in South Carolina, the advisory institutions that formed the other branch of the faith's Administrative Order also played important roles in the

Delegates from South Carolina in the gardens of the House of Worship, Bahá'í National Convention, Wilmette, Illinois, 1974. *From the* South Carolina Regional Bahá'í Bulletin.

planning and implementation of teaching, education, and the development of community identity. In late 1973, when the Universal House of Justice announced the increase in the number of Auxiliary Board members around the world, South Carolina was one of the areas that benefitted directly. Elizabeth Martin, a black high school English teacher who had moved with her husband and children to Winnsboro in 1968, was appointed to the Auxiliary Board for Propagation with responsibility for South Carolina. Previously, Auxiliary Board members in the Southeast had served a number of states; now one of them would have South Carolina alone on which to focus. During the rest of the decade, Martin worked closely with the regional and district teaching committees and the staff of the Louis Gregory Institute, conducted training seminars, helped organize conferences, wrote frequently for the state newsletter, and corresponded with and traveled extensively to local Bahá'í communities large and small.

More senior members of the faith's advisory institutions were present as well. Sarah Martin Pereira, appointed to the Continental Board of Counselors in 1973 after more than a decade of service on the National Spiritual Assembly, was a frequent visitor during the rest of the decade, and several Hands of the Cause of God, including 'Alí-Akbar Furútan, Zikrullah Khadem, Rahmatu'lláh Muhájir, John Robarts, and William Sears, made trips to the state, some of them more than once. In addition to their work in planning the teaching work and educating the community, the Hands of the Cause and Counselors who visited South Carolina played a more subtle

Auxiliary Board member Elizabeth Martin (*back row, fourth from left*) with Bahá'ís in Patrick, a small town in Chesterfield County, at a celebration of the formation of the town's Local Spiritual Assembly, 1978. *National Bahá'í Archives.*

but no less significant role in loving and encouraging those with whom they interacted. For example, a believer in Orangeburg, Emma Glover, recalled being visited in the hospital by Rahmatu'lláh Muhájir, who was a physician, after severely injuring her hand at work in 1976. Doctors had told her it would have to be amputated, but Muhájir sat by her bedside, stroked her hand, prayed with her, and assured her that it could be saved. Not only was the hand not amputated, but Glover also regained its full use, an outcome she attributed in part to Muhájir's kind intervention. Moreover, the fact that she, a local black woman, had received a visit from a "white" foreign dignitary caused people in the hospital to inquire about the faith.[88]

Approaches to Training

During the Five Year Plan, a variety of actors—including the staff and volunteers of the Louis Gregory Institute, various agencies of the National Spiritual Assembly, Auxiliary Board members, and the regional and district teaching committees—engaged in experimentation to try to discover the best ways to train large numbers of teachers and administrators for the South Carolina movement, to deepen the faith and strengthen the Bahá'í identity of thousands of believers, and to deploy human resources effectively in dozens of localities across the state. Their efforts were often thoughtful, energetic, and collaborative, and also sometimes chaotic and halting, resulting in a process that proved to be both immensely challenging and rewarding.

The center of experimentation with training and curriculum development was the Louis Gregory Institute. According to one early mission statement, its purpose was to train Bahá'í teachers and administrators and "to work with the national and regional teaching committees in coordinating the use of trained teachers in the field." In his remarks at the Institute's dedication program, Harold Jackson, its first dean, called the facility a "gift to the people of the South" that would have "aims, goals, and objectives, curriculum, lesson plans, and methods" designed specifically for them. However, the Institute began its life with no ready-made curriculum or training methods, no particular approach for recruiting participants from across the state, no system for deploying trained individuals for service in their home communities, and no roadmap for its working relationship with regional and district teaching committees. Moreover, frequent changes in administration likely made it difficult to take a long-term approach to the Institute's development. For example, in the middle of 1973, less than a year after the Institute's inauguration, Harold Jackson stepped down as dean to return to California to complete a graduate degree, and Bransford Watson, a former member of the National Teaching Committee, was appointed to take his place. The following summer, Caswell Ellis, a former manager of the House of Worship in Wilmette, was appointed assistant dean. Then in the spring of 1975, Allen Murray, a special education teacher and recent pioneer to the Charleston area, replaced Watson.[89]

In this context, the Institute experimented with a variety of programs, relying on volunteer instructors from around the state and elsewhere, and the results were somewhat haphazard. During 1974, the Institute began to offer a new five-day course, the Gregory Institute Intensive Deepening Program, almost weekly. Designed by the National Teaching Committee, it was intended primarily "to stimulate undeepened believers" and focused on the Covenant and the Administrative Order. Other programs of seven and nine days' duration were also held. By the end of 1976, the longer-form programs had mostly been replaced by three-day deepening weekends for new believers. During 1975, the Institute began to offer programs for children, in large part because the construction of a new classroom/dining hall building, divisible by folding walls into three sections, allowed for the holding of multiple concurrent programs. The Institute began regular weekly classes for local children, and during the summer, it held four weeklong sessions for children and two for youth, designed and supervised by Betty Morris, a Montessori teacher. The weekly class and the summer programs continued for several years.[90]

In addition to regular programs, the Institute also hosted Holy Day observances, community dinners, and youth activities that usually drew from a smaller geographic area, as well as occasional courses and seminars and special programs with attendees from across the state and region, such as a statewide youth conference in January 1975 that stretched the facilities to the limits. There also were occasions that fostered an appreciation of the South Carolina community's history and global connections, for example, a talk by Roy Williams of Greenville about his teaching trips across the region with Louis Gregory, and another by Vivian Wesson, a black Chicagoan who had helped establish new Bahá'í communities in Togo and Liberia during the Ten Year Plan. In fall 1975, the Institute received its first visit by a member

Early participants in the Louis Gregory Institute's programs, 1970s. *Louis G. Gregory Bahá'í Institute.*

Above and opposite: Early participants in the Louis Gregory Institute's programs, 1970s. *Louis G. Gregory Bahá'í Institute.*

of the Universal House of Justice. Hugh Chance, formerly the attorney for Palmer College of Chiropractic in Iowa, and his wife had taught the faith to a number of early homefront pioneers in the Pee Dee region. The Chances were guests of honor for the largest weekend gathering at the Institute since its opening, which included a campus workday and a traditional fish fry.[91]

By the end of the Five Year Plan, more than five years after the Institute's inauguration, there seemed to be a widespread consensus that raising up ranks of confident protagonists of the religion and promoting the social and spiritual transformation of individuals and communities had proven much harder than anyone had imagined. Yet the Institute had emerged as a vital center of learning and a site for strengthening bonds of community across the state and region. During a nine-month period in 1975–76 alone, after the completion of the new classroom building, the Institute served some 8,600 participants. Clearly, it had begun to affect the lives of thousands of people, even if there were thousands more whom its programs were unable to effectively reach.[92]

THE FOLLY GROVE COMMUNITY
AND OPPOSITION TO THE FAITH

An indirect benefit of the establishment of the Louis Gregory Institute
was the emergence of a vibrant local Bahá'í community in the immediate
surrounding area, a part of rural Georgetown County called Folly Grove.
Woodrow Jackson, an illiterate black farmer, was the first local resident to
become a Bahá'í, having befriended members of the Institute staff while
the facility was still under construction. He was followed by a number of his
family members and neighbors. Jackson's adult daughter, Mary Beckmon,
recalled investigating the Bahá'í Faith as a result of seeing the positive
transformation of local children participating in classes at the Institute.
Soon, members of the extended Jackson-Beckmon family were among the
most active supporters of the religion in the state. For example, in 1975,
Woodrow Jackson, who had never been outside the South, helped fulfill one
of the U.S. community's international goals for the Five Year Plan when he

Woodrow Jackson (1901–1997, *right*), the first person in the area around the Louis Gregory
Institute to become a Bahá'í, playing music with another believer, 1970s. A former
sharecropper with limited formal education, Jackson traveled to teach the faith across the
United States and in the Caribbean, often sharing his gifts on guitar and harmonica. *Louis
G. Gregory Bahá'í Institute.*

Serving a meal at the Louis Gregory Institute, late 1970s. *Left to right*: Mary Beckmon, Gwen Ellis-Cotton, Annette Young, Cindy Beckmon, Debbie Jackson, Moses Richardson, Barbara Pryor-Smith, Ursula Hoeller (later Richardson). Mary Beckmon (1941–2010) became a teacher and administrator of the faith, a cook at the Institute, and a noted song leader in the Bahá'í community. *Louis G. Gregory Bahá'í Institute*.

participated in a teaching trip to the Turks and Caicos Islands. Similarly, Mary Beckmon and her best friend and neighbor, Elnetha Graham, who had also become a Bahá'í, made trips to Jamaica and Trinidad. Beckmon, who had a fifth-grade education, served on her Local Spiritual Assembly, on the District Teaching Committee, and as a delegate to the National Convention. She became well known in the state and region as a singing leader and composer of Bahá'í songs and, as a cook at the Institute, for her traditional South Carolina cuisine.[93]

Beckmon also was among those targeted for violence and intimidation by local whites. During the 1970s, the Institute frequently received threatening phone calls, and vandals destroyed the mailbox on several occasions. Once, while she was walking to work at the Institute, a driver attempted to run Beckmon down, forcing her to jump into a roadside ditch. Across the state in the Piedmont town of York, pioneers Charles and Alice Nightingale, an interracial couple from Massachusetts, had a cross burned on their lawn, glass and nails scattered in their driveway, and "numerous obscene phone calls." As late as 1981 in Lydia, a hamlet in Darlington County near Florence, the

Above: Louis Gregory Institute mailbox damaged by gunshots, 1975. The vandalism was part of a pattern of white opposition to the theological and racial radicalism of the Bahá'í community. *From the* Weekly Observer *(Hemingway, SC)*.

Right: New believers from South Carolina visiting the Bahá'í House of Worship in Wilmette, Illinois, and their bus, damaged by a shotgun blast during a teaching project in a white neighborhood, 1971. *From the* American Bahá'í.

New Believers From South Carolina Visit House of Worship

About 30 friends from the Adams Run, Charleston and Dillon areas of South Carolina arrived one weekend recently in an old school bus painted blue and decorated on the sides with paintings of people from around the world with joined hands. The picture (right) shows the back of the bus scarred with shot-gun blasts which were fired during a teaching campaign in a white neighborhood where some people didn't take too kindly to the concept of the Oneness of Mankind. Fortunately, no one was hurt.

home of another interracial Bahá'í couple, Moses Richardson and his wife, Ursula, a German who had moved to South Carolina in 1976, was destroyed by arson. The pattern of harassment was familiar, going back to shortly after Louis Gregory's first teaching trip to the state. The incidents from Folly Grove, York, and Lydia indicate that in small-town South Carolina, the Bahá'ís' combination of unorthodox religious and racial views continued to make them targets of violence long after the passage of the Civil Rights Act of 1964.[94]

Approaches to Teaching

During the interim year and the Five Year Plan, Bahá'ís in South Carolina engaged in energetic experimentation in teaching. Sometimes their plans were grandiose and achieved much less than the desired results, with a measure of disappointment that the large-scale growth of the early part of the decade could not be replicated. For example, at a statewide conference at Penn Center in June 1973, the Regional Teaching Committee presented a five-month plan for the interim year that called for activating 3,000 of the state's Bahá'ís as teachers and enrolling 3,000 new believers. Presenting no specific program, the committee simply suggested that the ambitious goals would be reached if each Local Assembly in the state pledged to bring in 25 new declarants. Nevertheless, the conference participants decided to raise the goal to 6,000 new believers. At Thanksgiving, when some 250 people—half the number the committee had planned for, probably in large part because of the recent dramatic spike in gas prices due to the Arab oil embargo—gathered at the Wade Hampton Hotel in downtown Columbia for a conference to conclude the campaign, it was clear that the 6,000 new believers had failed to materialize. Yet a number of local initiatives had met with good results. For example, following a training seminar conducted by Helen Thomas, a veteran of the Dillon campaign, several summer youth projects had taken place, the most successful of which, in Rock Hill, had garnered 100 new believers, many of whom had arisen to help with the consolidation of others. In Greenwood and Saluda, the District Teaching Committee had experimented with a "Mobile Institute," a large van outfitted as a reading room, with materials for teaching, deepening, and holding children's classes, primarily to reach those who had become Bahá'ís in the area during the Army of Light project the previous year.[95]

After the conference, large and small local communities continued to pursue their own goals, illustrating a variety of approaches to expansion and consolidation. During late 1973 and early 1974 in Columbia, for example, the Local Spiritual Assembly planned a number of activities in Wheeler Hill, a mostly working-class black neighborhood adjacent to the University of South Carolina, including a "tent revival" program in February; thirteen people embraced the faith as a result. In the coastal city of Georgetown, a weekend project in March 1974 included newspaper and radio publicity and canvassing the city to deliver hundreds of invitations to a public meeting at the local library. Some seventy people attended the meeting, and two became Bahá'ís. In addition, during the course of the weekend, teachers met two people who had previously joined the faith but whose addresses had been lost.[96]

The pattern of successful local initiatives continued during the Five Year Plan itself. While the Regional Teaching Committee's statewide goals included several items related to expansion and the development of community life—including increasing the number of localities where Bahá'ís resided from three hundred to five hundred; forming eighty new, strong Local Spiritual Assemblies, with at least one in each county of the state; establishing children's classes in strong communities; and educating Local Assembly treasurers—there was no numerical goal for new believers, perhaps an admission of the failure of the five-month campaign. Nevertheless, many local communities responded energetically and creatively to the plan. For example, the Local Spiritual Assembly of Florence and the District Teaching Committee in the area worked together to coordinate a variety of teaching efforts in Florence and a number of surrounding towns. Another active community in the Pee Dee was Hartsville, a college town in Darlington County, where most of the Bahá'ís lived near one another in one neighborhood, and for a time, all the members of the Local Spiritual Assembly lived on the same street. Elizabeth Ellis, who had come from Vermont as a new Bahá'í for the Dillon campaign, stayed as a homefront pioneer, and married a local black believer, recalled a tight-knit Hartsville community in which virtually every gathering included food, singing, and socializing. The social portion of the Nineteen Day Feast often included a fish fry and card games late into the night.[97]

In the Piedmont, the Spartanburg community pursued a number of initiatives, including the acquisition of its first Bahá'í Center, a converted house in a predominantly African American neighborhood, in early 1975. A few months later, the area's District Teaching Committee sponsored a summer

Above: Local Bahá'ís and friends with homefront pioneers, black and white, at a public meeting in Saluda, 1974. *National Bahá'í Archives.*

Left: The "red record," a consolidation tool featuring songs from the southern teaching campaigns that was distributed to new Bahá'ís in South Carolina and elsewhere, circa 1970s. *Author's personal collection.*

youth project focusing on neighboring towns. Teachers opened Boiling Springs and Inman to the faith; in Union, where there was a list of believers but no organized activities, they "were greeted by friends who had been Bahá'ís for years and asked, 'Where have you been all this time?'" The visitors helped them to organize a group and elect officers in preparation for forming their Local Spiritual Assembly. The capstone of the project was a weekend trip for fourteen Spartanburg young people, most of them relatively new Bahá'ís, to the House of Worship in Wilmette—a powerful experience of cementing Bahá'í identity, strengthening bonds of community, and establishing spiritual and practical links with the national center of their faith.[98]

South Carolina and the National Plan

By the midpoint of the Five Year Plan, the Bahá'ís in South Carolina had made progress on a number of fronts. In South Carolina and in the country as a whole, however, there were no signs of the rapid membership growth of the early years of the decade, and the lack of progress in achieving the plan's domestic goals caused the National Spiritual Assembly considerable alarm. A significant number of Local Spiritual Assemblies formed late in the previous plan were now jeopardized due to low numbers, and the community was "lagging behind" its targets for the number of new localities opened and additional Local Assemblies established. Moreover, the "magnetic goal" of initiating entry by troops in California, Illinois, and New York seemed nowhere close to realization.[99]

In this context, the National Spiritual Assembly asked Hand of the Cause of God Rahmatu'lláh Muhájir to help plan a revival of large-scale growth in the South that would spark the necessary action across the country. The new program, which Muhájir announced at a large gathering at the Louis Gregory Institute in January 1976, called for large-scale teaching projects in the nine southern states that had nine or more Local Spiritual Assemblies. The National Teaching Committee would provide additional assistance for projects in and around Atlanta, Georgia; College Station, Texas; and Columbia, South Carolina. The initial results in South Carolina were modest but encouraging. By April 1976, some fifty people had become Bahá'ís across the state, with a notable uptick in teaching activities in Rock Hill and York, in the Columbia area, in Orangeburg, in Charleston and Beaufort, and in Florence and nearby towns. Notably, the number of children being served in Bahá'í classes doubled to some two hundred.[100]

Perhaps the most welcome boost in the opening phase of the new campaign came entirely unexpectedly. In March 1976, the jazz trumpeter John Birks "Dizzy" Gillespie, easily the most famous Bahá'í with South Carolina roots, was honored by the state government as part of its celebration of the national bicentennial. Born in Cheraw in 1917, Gillespie had grown up during the era of the boll weevil infestation and the brutal crackdown on the NAACP and moved with his family to Philadelphia in 1935. When he returned more than forty years later, he was an international star, having pioneered his own signature style, called "bebop," and collaborated with virtually all of the other leading jazz artists of his generation. Since becoming a Bahá'í in Los Angeles in 1968, he had been known for mentioning two things during his concerts: Cheraw (which he often jokingly pronounced "CHEE-raw") and the Bahá'í Faith. On March 9, Gillespie and his band performed for a joint session of the General Assembly—which had only welcomed its first African American members since Reconstruction in 1971—and guests, including Governor James B. Edwards and the mayor of Cheraw. During the ceremony, the South Carolina Arts Commission presented Gillespie with a plaque commending his contribution "to the world of music and the state of South Carolina." For his part, Gillespie said that he was "full of hope for America," quoting a short passage from 'Abdu'l-Bahá:

> *The continent of America is in the eyes of the one true God the land wherein the splendors of His light shall be revealed, where the mysteries of His Faith shall be unveiled, where the righteous will abide and the free assemble.*

Then he read the entire text of an editorial, "Two Hundred Years of Imperishable Hope," from the bicentennial issue of *World Order*, the National Spiritual Assembly's journal of ideas. Afterward, Governor Edwards hosted a reception for three hundred at a building in the Governor's Mansion complex, followed by a private dinner for Gillespie, his band, and members of the Arts Commission. It seemed a remarkable reversal of fortune for a black man who had fled his home state in search of dignity, security, and economic opportunity and a striking symbol of the extent to which the civil rights movement had revolutionized public life in South Carolina. And for a faith community whose religious radicalism and interracial commitment had left it struggling to achieve basic civil protections, much less public acceptance, since its arrival in the state, the occasion represented unprecedented recognition by South Carolina's government. Just blocks from where Alonzo Twine had died in 1914, the doors of the South Carolina State House and the Governor's Mansion had been opened, both literally and symbolically, to the Bahá'í Faith and its central principle of the oneness of humanity.[101]

While the Regional Teaching Committee's goals for the Five Year Plan in South Carolina envisioned the District Teaching Committees and stronger Local Spiritual Assemblies as the primary organizers of teaching—an approach that appeared only to be enhanced in the first few months of the new regional campaign—in June 1976, the staff of the Louis Gregory Institute proposed their own initiative to the Regional Teaching Committee. Named "Project Outreach," it called for teams of local and visiting teachers housed at the Institute to work full-time for the summer, with the goal of informing everyone within a thirty-mile radius of the campus about the faith.

John Birks "Dizzy" Gillespie (1917–1993), a native of Cheraw, performing for Governor Edwards and a joint session of the General Assembly as part of the state's official national bicentennial celebrations, South Carolina State House, Columbia, March 1976. Gillespie's likeness and that of fellow Bahá'í Dr. Ronald McNair (1950–1986) are recognizable on the African American Monument, installed on the State House grounds in 2001. *From* Bahá'í News.

A number of nearby towns and hamlets—Stuckey, Donnelly, and Nesmith in Williamsburg County, Gresham and Friendship in Marion County, and Andrews and Plantersville in Georgetown County—would receive special attention with a view to establishing a Local Spiritual Assembly in each. For the first several weeks, about a dozen mostly young Bahá'ís went out in teams to the focus communities every day. "We would walk down a road," one participant recalled, "and stop at each house, knocking on the door and handing the person an invitation" to activities at the Institute. If people asked questions, the teachers told them more about the faith. According to another participant, they "set up firesides in interested persons' homes as well as in new believers' homes," and sometimes they held classes for children. By focusing on a few small, rural neighborhoods over an extended period, the teachers were able to tap rich local networks of kinship and friendship to identify new seekers and to reestablish contact with people who had embraced the faith during previous campaigns.[102]

Unfortunately, the project soon fell prey to the same grandiosity that had led to the failure of the Regional Teaching Committee's five-month campaign in 1973. In mid-July, the secretary of the Regional Teaching Committee and a member of the National Teaching Committee came to the Institute to announce an entirely new approach. They said that the National Spiritual Assembly had decided to "give Project Outreach its unlimited support and an open-ended budget." The effort was to be broadened to a series of nine-week campaigns, with a goal to enroll 10,000 people in the first nine weeks. Soon the group was plagued by disagreements about leadership, goals, and methods, which even a visit by the secretary of the National Spiritual Assembly seemed unable to resolve. By the fall, most of the young volunteers had left to return to school, and Project Outreach quickly dwindled. Altogether, only about 110 people became Bahá'ís in the area during the summer, far short of the revised project's goal.[103]

After the failure of Project Outreach, the locus of planning shifted from the National Teaching Committee back to the regional and district committees. At a January 1977 meeting, the National Spiritual Assembly encouraged the South Carolina Bahá'ís to "initiate plans of their own and rely less on the National Center for guidance"—a somewhat strange directive given that it was the national agencies' imposition of Project Outreach, not the District Teaching Committees' lack of initiative, that had hampered the most recent effort. A new initiative, called "Operation Grassroots," envisioned expansion and consolidation work in each of the state's districts plus a concerted statewide media campaign including radio, television, and newspaper ads and direct mail. The results were modest, with a small number of enrollments around the state and the initiation of activities in a few new areas such as Cowpens and Gaffney, small towns near Spartanburg.[104]

In January 1978, the National Teaching Committee was back, with representatives at a meeting of 300 Bahá'ís from around the state, including 100 youth, to adopt a strategy for the remaining months of the Five Year Plan. Called simply "1000 + 80," it included goals of having 1,000 believers participating in community activities and 80 functioning Local Assemblies. The Universal House of Justice had announced that lapsed Local Spiritual Assemblies around the world could be reformed any time during the final year of the plan, and the strategy called for teams to visit every such locality in South Carolina. By the fall, dozens of

Above and opposite: Home visits, eastern South Carolina, 1979. During the 1970s, the practice of believers visiting one another's homes for prayer, study, and fellowship became a key element of the state's Bahá'í culture. *Personal collection of Sandy Hoover*.

localities had received multiple visits, resulting in the enrollment of new believers as well as reconnecting with older ones. In Marion, for example, where no teachers had visited in at least two years, one team reported finding that the believers were keeping up with national and international news in the *American Bahá'í*. Trudy White, the committee's secretary, noted that many communities would gladly receive more visits, but there were too few teachers and too few cars available. All of the state's districts but one exceeded their goals for the formation of Local Assemblies and the opening of new localities, some by wide margins. In November, the National Spiritual Assembly announced that the national community had reached its Five Year Plan goal of 1,400 Local Assemblies, aided in no small part by the effort in South Carolina.[105]

The Seven Year Plan (1979–1986), Project Tabarsi and Radio Bahá'í

During the next global teaching plan, begun in 1979 and set to last for seven years, the maintenance and strengthening of new Local Spiritual Assemblies remained a challenge across the country, and the goal of starting large-scale enrollments outside the Deep South remained elusive. In other ways, however, the early 1980s witnessed important strides forward for the national Bahá'í movement. In South Carolina, the Seven Year Plan was marked by substantial accomplishments in the areas of expansion and consolidation, public relations, and social and economic development—including the establishment of the religion's first radio station in North America on the campus of the Louis Gregory Institute.

Late in 1982, the National Assembly announced that the Federal Communications Commission had granted a license for a fifty-thousand-watt, noncommercial radio station at the Louis Gregory Institute. Under the call letters WLGI, it would broadcast uplifting music, information about the faith for seekers and believers, and programs designed to foster the area's social and economic development. Individuals and local communities in South Carolina and across the country engaged in creative fundraising to build the $1 million endowment that the National Spiritual Assembly said was needed to open the station. By January 1984, the goal had been exceeded, and construction of the radio tower was completed two months later. The station's maiden broadcast—a taped statement by Hand of the

Cause of God William Sears, a former radio and television personality—took place on May 23, the anniversary of the Declaration of the Báb. Technical challenges forced a formal dedication ceremony to be delayed until the following spring. Six hundred people attended the event, broadcast live by the station, in March 1985, including Ruth Pringle, a member of the Continental Board of Counselors living in Panama, all nine members of the National Spiritual Assembly, and a number of state and local political leaders. The station was only the most visible of a number of initiatives in social and economic development, inspired in part by a letter from the Universal House of Justice on the subject in 1983, undertaken in the state during the 1980s. These included the Black Men's Gathering, an annual conference of African American men seeking to overcome the effects of racism and contribute to the work of the Bahá'í community; the Children's and Youth Academies, residential summer programs at the Institute that combined social, academic, and spiritual training and service; the North Family Community School, a literacy center in Orangeburg County; a clothing bank housed in the bakery of new believers in Loris, near Conway; and a number of small initiatives in agriculture.[106]

Transmission tower of Radio Bahá'í WLGI, the radio station at the Louis Gregory Institute, prior to installation, 1984. *Louis G. Gregory Bahá'í Institute.*

The effort to establish WLGI—an important step in building public awareness of the religion and in consolidating new Bahá'ís more than a decade in the making—coincided with a renewed push to enroll larger numbers of new believers spearheaded by the District Teaching Committee serving the Florence area. In early 1982, for example, some 550 people became Bahá'ís during a nine-day project, including about one-third of the residents of the hamlet of Lydia in Darlington County. A summer project in July 1984 mobilized more than 100 young Bahá'ís for teaching in 20 localities, with consolidation visits to dozens of homes and 30 declarations. The following spring, the committee prepared for a larger project in collaboration with the Louis Gregory Institute and the Regional Teaching Committee. Launched at a conference at the Institute in April 1985, the project took its name from the siege of Fort Tabarsi, a key event in the early history of the faith in which several hundred of the Báb's followers in Iran withstood an eleven-month siege by soldiers of the shah. Project Tabarsi would also last eleven months, from June 1985 until the end of the Seven Year Plan in May 1986. The approach was to select a limited number of localities where the faith was already established for "saturation teaching," that is, bringing the faith to "whole groups of people, families and neighborhoods" in order to create a stronger base of "mutual support" and provide for more effective consolidation. During the first two months, teams of teachers enrolled 1,500 new believers, the largest burst of growth in the country since 1972.[107]

As in previous efforts, music and the arts played important roles in Project Tabarsi. The Bahá'í Youth Workshop, a performing arts troupe from Los Angeles, participated for several weeks during the summer, performing for hundreds of people "on the streets, in churches, at schools, and at the Myrtle Beach shopping mall." For example, nearly three hundred people attended a performance in Lake City, of whom eighty-seven became Bahá'ís. In addition to introducing the faith's teachings directly to audiences, the interracial company also garnered extensive local media coverage. In contrast to previous initiatives, this time teachers had a radio station at their disposal. WLGI was a "constant presence" in expansion, advertising performances and public meetings in advance, as well as in consolidation, helping new believers "mold their Bahá'í identities through exposure to prayers…the principles of the Faith, and the schedule of…Feasts and Holy Days." Drawing from previous experience, teachers in Project Tabarsi often focused on consolidation, even during their initial meeting with new believers, encouraging them to pray and teach and giving them copies of the Bahá'í writings. One of the books, a new volume titled *Bahá'í Day Book*, was designed to facilitate reading of the scriptures "every morn and eve," a spiritual practice ordained by Bahá'u'lláh. New believers also began to receive an attractive new bulletin prepared by the Regional Teaching Committee, with features on the laws, teachings, and history of the faith; news from around the state; and information about the Louis Gregory Institute and WLGI.[108]

Another new element of consolidation was the use of training materials developed during the previous decade in Colombia. Inspired in part by the original upsurge of large-scale growth in South Carolina in 1970–71, the Colombian Bahá'í community had set out on a similar path of teaching in rural areas. Facing their own consolidation needs, groups of Bahá'ís had developed a series of short courses for new believers through an agency of the national community called the Ruhi Institute. With an emphasis on studying and memorizing relevant passages from the faith's scriptures, the courses focused on developing the participants' knowledge and skills for service in a growing community, for example, by making home deepening visits to other new believers and teaching a series of simple classes for children. Farzam

Cap Cornwell, secretary of the National Teaching Committee, wearing a WLGI T-shirt while participating in Project Tabarsi in Kingstree, 1986. *National Bahá'í Archives.*

Arbab, a member of the Continental Board of Counselors and one of the developers of the curriculum, arranged for a trainer to come from Colombia to prepare an initial group in South Carolina to offer the courses. They began regular meetings to study the materials with groups of local youth, most of them new believers, in several towns across the state.[109]

By the end of Project Tabarsi, some 2,500 people had become Bahá'ís in South Carolina, the state counted 265 Local Spiritual Assemblies (more than California), and important improvements in consolidation appeared to be taking place. However, there were developments in other areas as well. In 1979, the Islamic Revolution that began in Iran unleashed an orgy of violence against the Bahá'ís, the country's largest religious minority. The Universal House of Justice directed national Bahá'í communities around the world not only to take steps to welcome Iranian Bahá'í refugees but also to make energetic representations to their respective governments to ask for help in mitigating the persecution.

Greenville mayor William Workman (*right*) presenting local Bahá'ís Richard Shurcliffe (*left*) and Charles Abercrombie (*center*) with a city council resolution condemning the persecution of Bahá'ís in Iran, 1985. The wave of oppression and violence unleashed by the Islamic Revolution of 1979 led to unprecedented public attention to the faith around the world, including South Carolina. *National Bahá'í Archives.*

Morrisville Brass Band, a local group, performing in the main tent at Peace Fest, Louis Gregory Institute, 1990s. *Louis G. Gregory Bahá'í Institute.*

In the United States, this resulted in extensive contact with federal and state officials and more attention from the media about the beliefs and practices of the Bahá'í community than ever before. In South Carolina, the Local Spiritual Assembly of Charleston was tasked with arranging for a resolution of the General Assembly condemning the persecution of the Iranian Bahá'ís, and city councils in Florence, Greenville, and other localities passed similar resolutions.[110]

Additional opportunities for raising the public profile of the faith came in 1985, designated by the United Nations as the "International Year of Peace," when the Universal House of Justice published a major statement titled *The Promise of World Peace.* Addressed to "the peoples of the world," the document looked beyond the Cold War to lay out a number of principles and elements essential to building the architecture of a new global order—including, for example, eliminating prejudices based on race, religion, and sex; redressing global disparities in access to wealth and education; and tempering unfettered nationalism. In June 1986, as part of a global campaign to distribute the document to political leaders, a delegation of five South Carolina Bahá'ís presented it to Governor Richard W. Riley (a future U.S. secretary of education), and local communities around the state made similar presentations to county and municipal officials. For the staff of the Louis Gregory Institute and the radio station and local Bahá'ís in the Pee Dee, the statement inspired a new initiative to build relationships with their neighbors. Peace Fest, a two-day celebration on the grounds of the Institute, was held in mid-September 1986. The event drew hundreds of people and featured a variety of musical performers, including Dizzy Gillespie and a jazz band he assembled for the occasion and a "Gospel Jubilee" featuring local groups. A "Peace Forum" included a keynote address by Reverend McKinley Young, pastor of historic Big Bethel AME Church in Atlanta, and a panel discussion of journalists, academics, and activists from across the state. The event was so successful that it was repeated every fall for the next quarter century.[111]

THE SIX YEAR PLAN, THE HOLY YEAR AND THE THREE YEAR PLAN (1986–1996)

In the decade following Project Tabarsi, the American Bahá'í community engaged in a Six Year Plan (1986–92) and a Three Year Plan (1993–96), separated by a Holy Year designated by the Universal House of Justice to commemorate the centenary of Bahá'u'lláh's death and the passing of authority to 'Abdu'l-Bahá. While marked by several significant developments for the Bahá'í Faith worldwide—including the reestablishment of the religion in the former Soviet bloc after the sudden end of the Cold War—in the United States, the period was one of much less rapid membership growth than the previous plans. In South Carolina, there was significant consolidation of local Bahá'í communities, especially in and around the state's metropolitan areas, and Bahá'í individuals and groups continued to contribute to the life of society. However, after the last surge of large-scale growth during Project Tabarsi, the momentum of teaching and community development in many smaller towns and rural areas declined significantly.

Near the beginning of the Six Year Plan, in August 1987, the Universal House of Justice announced its intention to complete the construction of the Bahá'í World Center on Mount Carmel in Haifa. The massive undertaking would include a kilometer-long series of garden terraces above and below the Shrine of the Báb and two new administrative buildings, the seat of the International Teaching Center and the Center for the Study of the Texts, on the arc-shaped path adjacent to the seat of the Universal House of Justice and the International Baháʼí Archives. The House of Justice called for an initial sum of $50 million to start what came to be called the "Arc Project," plus an additional $20 to $25 million annually for a decade to finish it. Given the situation of the Iranian Baháʼís, the bulk of the financial burden would fall on the United States, but the National Spiritual Assembly doubted whether it could raise the huge and unexpected sums required without a significant influx of new Baháʼís. In 1988, it announced a series of twelve conferences, including one in Columbia, South Carolina, to explore the "challenges" of completing the Arc Project and of "initiating the process of entry by troops." The results were mixed. Throughout the Six Year Plan, enrollments remained steady but low, while contributions to the Arc Project gradually rose, in part through community fundraising events that became common in South Carolina and across the country.[112]

At the Louis Gregory Institute, an unexpected opportunity to serve the community and build bonds of trust with neighbors came in October 1989 when Hurricane Hugo, the most damaging storm to hit the United States up to that time, devastated portions of the South Carolina coast. Property damage was extensive, and many areas were without electricity or water for days. WLGI broadcast detailed information from prior to landfall until its transmitter went down, and shortly after the storm passed, the Institute campus became a center for relief distribution in the rural area around Hemingway. Building on the relationships that had been cultivated since the inauguration of Peace Fest three years earlier, staff members recalled that people who never would have set foot on the campus before now came to receive assistance. After the hurricane, area Baháʼís had the impression that they had turned a corner in local public relations; no longer would they be perceived as outsiders or as a threat but as part of the community.[113]

In 1991, the National Spiritual Assembly, picking up one of the themes in the statement on peace by the Universal House of Justice, issued its own public statement titled "The Vision of Race Unity: America's Most Challenging Issue." Deploring a resurgence of racial incidents and "the deepening despair of minorities and the poor," it called on all Americans of goodwill to act boldly to root out racism, and it offered the experience of the Baháʼí community as a model for others to study. In South Carolina, the document provided further impetus to a number of local efforts to promote interracial unity. In Greenville, for example, the community sponsored annual programs for both Martin Luther King Day and Black History Month, and the Spartanburg community co-sponsored an annual King Day celebration with the local Human Relations Commission. In Conway, nine-year-old Anisa Kintz gathered a group of friends to organize a children's conference on racism, named "Calling All Colors" and sponsored by Coastal Carolina University. The conference garnered coverage in several newspapers around the state, and in February 1992, Kintz was honored for her work by a resolution of the South Carolina General Assembly. In April—just before the Rodney King riots in Los Angeles dramatically illustrated the relevance of the National Assembly's statement—President George H.W. Bush named her a "Daily Point of Light."[114]

The hallmarks of the Holy Year were two major commemorative events, both of which included significant participation by South Carolinians. The first, held in May 1992 at the Bahá'í World Center, was a solemn

Hurricane Hugo relief, Louis Gregory Institute, September 1989. Local white opposition to the Bahá'í community softened significantly after the Institute staff opened the facility to disaster relief services. *Louis G. Gregory Bahá'í Institute.*

commemoration of the 100th anniversary of Bahá'u'lláh's passing. The participants included delegations from every national Bahá'í community and all the living "Knights of Bahá'u'lláh"—the first pioneers to a country or territory designated during the Ten Year Plan. Among the nineteen-member U.S. delegation appointed by the National Spiritual Assembly were Charles Abercrombie of Greenville and Eulalia Bobo, who had helped lay the foundation for large-scale growth in South Carolina as a traveling teacher in the 1960s. Also attending from South Carolina were two Knights of Bahá'u'lláh, Gerald and Gail Curwin, pioneers in Greenwood since the 1970s who had earlier been among the first Bahá'ís to settle in the Bahamas. The second event, held in November in New York City, was the Second Bahá'í World Congress. Dozens of South Carolinians attended, and several sang in the choirs assembled for the occasion—including a gospel choir featuring pieces by Bahá'í composers, a testimony to the cultural shift in the American Bahá'í community in the wake of large-scale growth in the Deep South.[115]

Calling All Colors conference, Conway, 1991. *Coastal Carolina University.*

Like the Six Year Plan before it, the Three Year Plan (1993–1996) witnessed a great deal of activity with little numerical growth, a fact that distressed the National Spiritual Assembly. This led to an unprecedented invitation for the entire body of the National Assembly to come to the World Center for several days of consultation with the Universal House of Justice. In a lengthy follow-up letter addressing a number of the concerns the National Assembly had raised, the House of Justice indicated that an "over-anxiousness" about the persistent trend of low enrollments in the United States and an "undue worry over the state of society" could be "counter-productive." The House of Justice wrote that the Bahá'ís were sowing seeds, and with the further breakdown of society in the years ahead they would certainly bear more fruit. Regarding the National Assembly's concern that over-centralization of the Bahá'í administration was stifling individual initiative in the country, the House of Justice essentially concurred. Warning that the "corrosive influence

Six members of the National Spiritual Assembly of the Bahá'ís of the United States, including South Carolina residents Alberta Deas (*third from right*), Jack McCants (*second from right*) and Tod Ewing (*far right*), Bahá'í International Convention, Haifa, Israel, 1993. Louis Gregory served on the National Assembly and its predecessor organization a total of sixteen years between 1912 and 1946. *National Bahá'í Archives.*

of an overbearing and rampant secularization is infecting the style of administration of the Faith in your community and threatening to undermine its efficacy," it called the members of the National Assembly to manifest unity and humility and, beyond the setting of goals, asked them to learn how to make use of people's talents and arouse the mass of the believers "in fulfillment of such goals." In retrospect, it appears that a number of the challenges that the next global plan was meant to address had already become clear to the Universal House of Justice.[116]

"A New State of Mind"

Reorganization and Renewal, 1996–2010

In the mid-1990s, after more than thirty years' worth of experience with large-scale growth in various countries, the Universal House of Justice launched a new series of global plans with a single focus: to achieve "a significant advance in the process of entry by troops" in every national community. Regardless of their prior experiences or current circumstances, the House of Justice stated, Bahá'í communities everywhere would have to prepare themselves for accelerated growth, work "towards embracing masses of new believers," and set in motion "the means for effecting their spiritual and administrative training and development." The key to the new effort would be the development of a worldwide network of training institutes, agencies that would offer educational programs designed to "endow ever-growing contingents of believers with the spiritual insights, knowledge, and skills needed to carry out the many tasks of expansion and consolidation, including the teaching and deepening of a large number of people—adults, youth, and children."[117]

In South Carolina, where the last attempt at large-scale growth had ended a decade earlier, the news was welcomed by those who looked for a return to the impressive growth of the past but with more effective means of consolidation. However, for others in the state and in the national community as a whole—who had not experienced previous episodes of large-scale growth directly, understood it poorly, or were simply focused on other concerns—even "spiritually and mentally accepting the possibility" of entry by troops proved immensely challenging. South Carolina, arguably the place with the most to gain from implementing the new guidance of the House of Justice, thus found itself again at the center of major changes in the priorities of the American Bahá'í movement.[118]

The Four Year Plan, the Twelve Month Plan and the Training Institute (1996–2001)

In preparation for launching a Four Year Plan at Ridván 1996, the Universal House of Justice offered an assessment of previous approaches to training that seemed a perfect summary of experiences in South Carolina:

> *During the Nine Year Plan, the Universal House of Justice called upon National Spiritual Assemblies in countries where large-scale expansion was taking place to establish teaching institutes to meet the deepening needs of the thousands who were entering the Faith. At that time, the emphasis was on acquiring a physical facility to which group after group of newly enrolled believers would be invited to attend deepening courses. Over the years, in conjunction with these institutes, and often independent of them, a number of courses—referred to, for example, as weekend institutes, five-day institutes, and nine-day institutes—were developed for the purpose of helping the friends gain an understanding of the fundamental verities of the Faith and arise to serve it.*

Such efforts had been worthwhile, but they had been inadequate to the magnitude of the challenge:

> *With the growth in the number of enrollments, it has become apparent that such occasional courses of instruction and the informal activities of community life, though important, are not sufficient as a means of human resource development, for they have resulted in only a relatively small band of active supporters of the Cause. These believers, no matter how dedicated, no matter how willing to make sacrifices, cannot attend to the needs of hundreds, much less thousands, of fledgling local communities.*

In order to develop human resources for the work of the faith "on a large scale," the House of Justice stated, such institutes would have to be "viewed in a new light." Rather than thinking of them primarily as physical facilities with a range of programs conducted in one location—the model of the Louis Gregory Institute—the new "training institutes" should be seen as "organizational structures" with a "well-defined program" of "regular training courses" offered "both at a central location and in the villages and towns so that an appreciable number of believers can enter its programs." Training institutes would be agencies of the National Spiritual Assembly, with large countries perhaps having several to cover their territory, and each National Assembly was left with a great deal of latitude to experiment with materials, methods, and organization.[119]

In the United States, the National Spiritual Assembly initially encouraged Local Spiritual Assemblies and groups of interested individuals to develop materials and establish their own training institutes, and several individuals and institutions in South Carolina were among those who attempted to do so. At the same time, agencies of the National Assembly also created materials that were disseminated nationally through seminars at Louhelen Bahá'í School in Michigan and elsewhere. After this somewhat chaotic start, the National Assembly began to establish a number of training institutes more along the lines of the new model, including one to serve South Carolina. By the second half of the plan, the board of directors of the new South Carolina institute had begun to offer courses, mostly as weekend programs, using some locally produced materials and parts of the Ruhi Institute curriculum that had first been used in the state during Project Tabarsi. About the same time, the International Teaching Center began to encourage institutes everywhere to decentralize their offerings via study circles, groups of some "six to ten believers in the towns and villages throughout the country, who will go through a series of basic courses together with a tutor," an individual who had already taken the courses and received some training in facilitating their study.[120]

The establishment of training institutes was not the only major administrative development that profoundly affected the South Carolina community during the Four Year Plan. Another structural change came with the introduction of Regional Bahá'í Councils, a new elected institution between the local and national levels introduced by the Universal House of Justice. Starting in 1985 in India, where the Bahá'í community had grown to more than one million people, the House of Justice had encouraged several National Spiritual Assemblies serving large territories to experiment with forming elected or appointed regional bodies. In the United States, which had tried virtually every possible national and regional committee structure since the 1930s, the National Assembly decided in

1996 to disband all the country's District Teaching Committees (as well as the state committee still serving South Carolina) and to reestablish four regional teaching committees. In early 1997, the Universal House of Justice announced the creation of the new institution of the Regional Bahá'í Council and its gradual introduction as conditions in various countries warranted. The new regional committees in the United States, it specified, would be quickly converted into Regional Bahá'í Councils, each with nine members elected by the Local Spiritual Assemblies in its jurisdiction beginning the following November. The new Regional Councils quickly assumed supervision of the training institutes in their respective areas and began to formulate teaching plans. Among the first actions of the new Regional Bahá'í Council of the Southern States was to meet in Columbia with members of South Carolina's Local Spiritual Assemblies in order to introduce itself and encourage a revival of teaching in the state. It also briefly experimented with appointing subsidiary teaching committees, including a statewide one for South Carolina and another just for the WLGI listening area. The members of the latter committee chose Lake City in Florence County, with more than two hundred people on the local membership list, as the focus of their efforts. They visited everyone on the list at least once, finding that the vast majority of people still identified themselves as believers and expressed openness to participating in Bahá'í community life. With financial support from the Regional Council and individuals in the area, they opened a Bahá'í Center in a rented storefront on Main Street and held a "tent revival" featuring participation by the choir of the Louis Gregory Institute. Despite the initially encouraging results, with the training institute still in its infancy, there was little prospect of Lake City residents themselves leading a revitalization of the local Bahá'í community.[121]

Another decision of the Universal House of Justice that directly affected South Carolina concerned the election of Local Spiritual Assemblies. For twenty years, it had permitted Local Assemblies in areas that had experienced large-scale growth to be elected at any point during the twelve-day Festival of Riḍván, a policy that had "enabled the believers in a large number of localities to receive assistance in electing their Local Spiritual Assemblies." Starting in 1997, however, all Local Assemblies, regardless of location, would have to be elected on the first day of the festival. The House of Justice anticipated an immediate drop in the total number of Local Assemblies but predicted that as the programs of the training institutes reached more and more areas, the number would gradually rise. It specified that National Assemblies and the Counselors and their auxiliaries could best discharge their responsibility to foster the development of Local Spiritual Assemblies by fully implementing the "sustained educational programs" that it had called for, which would "create in the believers the awareness of the importance of the Teachings in every area of their individual and social lives and…engender in them the desire and determination to elect and support their Local Spiritual Assemblies." In South Carolina, however, with a weak training institute and no other agency focused on the issue, the number of Local Assemblies indeed dropped precipitously, from 168 in 1996 to 49 in 1997. By the turn of the century, with some 35 Local Assemblies mostly clustered in metropolitan areas, the Bahá'í Faith had no more institutional presence, even on paper, in vast stretches of rural South Carolina.[122]

While the results in South Carolina and the rest of the United States were modest, by the end of the Four Year Plan, the Universal House of Justice could state that in global perspective, it had represented a "major advance on those that immediately preceded it." Most notably, the establishment of a worldwide network of some three hundred training institutes had resulted in a marked change in the culture of the community. Adopting a "learning mode," Bahá'í individuals, institutions, and communities were increasingly able to deepen their knowledge of the faith's teachings and apply them to vital questions of teaching, administration, and "working with their neighbors." Building on this success, the Universal House of Justice announced a brief Twelve Month Plan aimed at "concentrating the forces, the capacities, and the insights" that had just emerged, to be followed by a series of plans to "carry the Bahá'í community through the final twenty years in the first century of the Faith's Formative Age" and ending in 2021. During the Twelve Month Plan, training institutes were to "bring into full operation" their programs, with particular attention on training teachers of children's classes, while the International Teaching Center would collaborate with selected National Spiritual Assemblies to establish a few "Area Growth Programs" on each continent. The purpose of the latter initiative was to field test what the International Teaching Center had identified as "certain patterns of systematic expansion and consolidation for relatively small geographical areas consisting of a manageable number of localities." Despite a request by the Regional Bahá'í Council of the Southern States to be included, no area in the United States was chosen to be part of the experiment.[123]

The Five Year Plan and a "Change in Time" (2001–2006)

The conclusion of the Twelve Month Plan and the opening of a new Five Year Plan were punctuated by two landmark events, both attended by South Carolinians, at the Bahá'í World Center. The events came at what the Universal House of Justice called a "change in time": in the world at large, the conclusion of a decade that had witnessed remarkable strides toward world peace and the start of a new millennium, and within the Bahá'í community, evidence that a "new state of mind" had everywhere taken root since the start of the Four Year Plan. The first event, held in January 2001, was an unprecedented global conference of the Institution of the Counselors—comprising the International Teaching Center, the Continental Boards of Counselors, and more than 800 Auxiliary Board members residing in 172 countries—to mark the inauguration of the new seat of the International Teaching Center and prepare for the upcoming plan. Noting that the quality of their deliberations signaled a new stage in the faith's administrative development, at the close of the conference the House of Justice announced that the faith had entered the fifth epoch of its Formative Age.

The second event, held the following May, marked the public dedication of the nineteen garden terraces of the Shrine of the Báb. With their opening, the Arc Project begun in 1987 was finished, and the faith's World Center was essentially complete. Among the nineteen representatives allotted to the U.S. Bahá'í community was Trudy White, an important figure in teaching and administration in South Carolina since the 1970s. Her selection by the National Spiritual Assembly was a testimony to the pivotal role the state had played in the development of the faith in the United States.[124]

Setting the stage for the new Five Year Plan, the Universal House of Justice explained that since 1996 not only had the massive construction projects on Mount Carmel been completed, but the capacity of the Bahá'í community to sustain large-scale growth had also increased significantly through the establishment of Regional Councils and particularly of training institutes. Now, based on the experience of conducting teaching projects in small geographic areas during the Twelve Month Plan, the Universal House of Justice introduced another new concept. The Counselors and National Spiritual Assemblies were to divide the entire territory of each country into geographic clusters according to basic social, economic, and demographic patterns, for example, a group of nearby towns and villages or a large city

Participants in the conference of the Institution of the Counselors visiting the new seat of the International Teaching Center, Haifa, Israel, January 2001. Annette Reynolds, a Darlington native and one of two Auxiliary Board members from South Carolina in attendance, recalled her sense of "awe, wonderment, and privilege" to be there. *Bahá'í World News Service*.

Beverly Abercrombie of Greenville, a staff member of the Bahá'í World Center, singing with a choir from the Democratic Republic of the Congo at the opening of the terraces of the Shrine of the Báb, May 2001. *Bahá'í World News Service.*

and its suburbs. Henceforth, the principal focus of national and regional plans would be to make provisions for opening clusters with no Bahá'ís through the settlement of pioneers, strengthening those where the faith was established but not yet ready for large-scale growth, and, in the strongest ones, beginning programs of "systematic and accelerated expansion and consolidation."[125]

Focusing on "a few methods that have proven over the years to be indispensable to large-scale expansion and consolidation," intensive programs of growth in the most advanced clusters would involve the close collaboration of the training institute, the Auxiliary Board members and

Dedication ceremony of the terraces of the Shrine of the Báb, May 2001. The opening of the garden terraces, stretching a kilometer above and below the Shrine on the north face of Mount Carmel, marked the completion of the Arc Project started in 1987. *Bahá'í World News Service*.

their assistants, and an Area Teaching Committee similar in purpose to the previous District Teaching Committees in the United States. As the number of new believers rose through individual teaching efforts and well-organized collective campaigns, a "significant percentage" of them would receive training from the institute and begin to contribute in turn to the process of community development. In addition to the strengthening of Local Spiritual Assemblies and observance of the Nineteen Day Feast, objectives that had loomed large in previous plans since the 1970s, communities would consider among their "initial goals" the establishment of study circles, classes for children, and devotional meetings "open to all the inhabitants of the locality." Plans should be formulated locally for a few months at a time, with all those involved in their implementation meeting periodically to "reflect on issues, consider adjustments, and maintain enthusiasm and unity of thought."[126]

In response to the new guidance, the Regional Bahá'í Council of the Southern States divided the region into clusters, twenty of which lay all or partly in South Carolina. Most comprised two or more counties, smaller in size than the previous teaching districts. The Council also modified the region's training institute structure, merging the three institutes in North

Some of the participants in a training in Book 7 of the Ruhi Institute curriculum, *Walking Together on a Path of Service*, Florence Bahá'í Center, 2003. *Personal collection of Greg and Ginny Kintz.*

Carolina, South Carolina, and Georgia into a single entity with one board of directors and a full-time Regional Coordinator. By 2002, the Carolinas and Georgia Regional Training Institute was conducting training programs in more than sixty clusters, and the number of devotional meetings and children's classes—the activities most closely associated with study of the first and third books of the Ruhi Institute's sequence of courses—began to rise in several areas. Early in the plan, a new course to prepare tutors of study circles became widely available, and the training institute and the Auxiliary Board members arranged to offer it in several clusters in South Carolina, including areas where Bahá'í community life had waned. In 2003, the Regional Council judged four areas of the Carolinas and Georgia—including the Greater Columbia cluster in South Carolina, composed of Lexington and Richland Counties—to be sufficiently strong to launch intensive programs of growth during the Five Year Plan. In Columbia, as elsewhere across the region, the growth was miniscule compared to that of the early 1970s, measured in the tens rather than the thousands. However, early evidence indicated that new believers were integrating more seamlessly than before into a vibrant community life and, through participation in the courses of the training institute, arising as confident teachers themselves. Moreover, the number of people who, while not enrolling in the faith, participated in the community's activities, rose appreciably.[127]

The Louis Gregory Museum

Near the mid-point of the Five Year Plan in February 2003, approximately 300 people from South Carolina and elsewhere gathered to dedicate Louis Gregory's childhood home in downtown Charleston as a museum. The three-day program was the culmination of more than a decade's worth of local effort proceeding parallel to the faith's global administrative restructuring. Louis Gregory's stepfather had built the modest, two-story house—an example of the classic Charleston "single house," with a long side porch and a narrow façade facing the street—for his family in the mid-1880s. More than a century later it had long since passed from the family's hands and was in need of major repairs. Charleston's Local Spiritual Assembly purchased the property in 1989 and began to raise money to restore the house, with significant assistance arriving from Bahá'ís around the state and across the country. At the same time the local community accumulated a

Louis G. Gregory Bahá'í Museum, Charleston. Acquired serendipitously in 1989, the building took more than a decade to restore and open to the public. The museum's sign was made by Philip Simmons (1912–2009), noted keeper of Charleston's wrought-iron tradition. *Author's personal collection.*

collection of documents, photographs, and artifacts relating to Gregory's life and career. Public historian Curtis Franks, curator at the College of Charleston's Avery Research Center for African American History and Culture—the former Avery Institute, Louis Gregory's alma mater—helped prepare the community's collection for display, and Philip Simmons, a local master blacksmith and noted keeper of Charleston's distinctive wrought-iron tradition, crafted the museum's sign.[128]

Soon the Louis G. Gregory Bahá'í Museum was welcoming the public, although the local community's relatively small resources meant that it was usually open by appointment only. Nevertheless, the museum represented a significant step in public relations for South Carolina's Bahá'ís. Nearly a century after the faith's arrival in the state, the South Carolina community had acquired, restored, and opened to the public a historic site associated with the life of its "founding father." It was also an important moment for Charleston itself. In a virtual city of museums, the Louis Gregory Museum was the first one dedicated to the life of a single individual.[129]

Another Five Year Plan and "Youth Taking Their Rightful Place" (2006–2011)

By the end of the Five Year Plan, the Universal House of Justice could say that it had been an important breakthrough for a global community that had been grappling with the implications of mass teaching since the 1960s. "Never before," wrote the House of Justice, "have the means for establishing a pattern of activity that places equal emphasis on the twin processes of expansion and consolidation been better understood." During the course of the plan, Bahá'ís around the world had gained an appreciation for the value of the training institute process, had learned to think about the growth of the faith on a manageable geographical scale, and had become more adept at analyzing the lessons they were learning. The elements of the new strategy for promoting the process of entry by troops had "crystalized," according to the House of Justice, "into a framework for action that…need[ed] only to be exploited." During the course of the plan, some 200 clusters around the world had established intensive programs of growth; during a new five-year effort starting in 2006 at least 1,500 more would be established, with 10 clusters lying all or partly in South Carolina, identified by the Regional Bahá'í Council, part of that total.[130]

The second Five Year Plan began with two important modifications to the training institute system. First, the Universal House of Justice added junior youth groups—the fruit of pilot programs designed both to improve literacy and foster moral decision-making among middle school–aged young people—to the core activities of devotional gatherings, children's classes, and study circles to be established in every cluster. Second, it directed that the "books of the Ruhi Institute should constitute the main sequence of courses for institutes everywhere." Most national communities had adopted this curriculum during the Four Year Plan, and those that had implemented

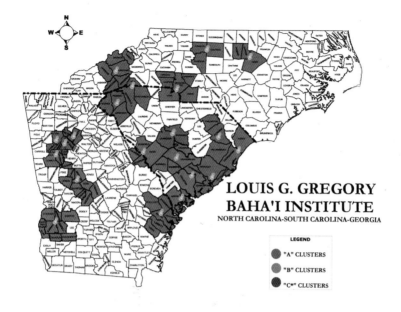

Geographic clusters in the Carolinas and Georgia slated for the establishment of intensive programs of growth during the Five Year Plan, 2007. *Author's personal collection.*

it "vigorously" had come out "far ahead of those who had attempted to develop their own program." Other materials developed over the years, the House of Justice noted, might still be useful for local deepening classes or eventually modified to form a specialized "branch" of the main sequence of courses. The immediate need, however, was for every national community to fully implement the curriculum that had proven to be the most effective in a variety of circumstances. The House of Justice also made clear that while individual Bahá'ís were not required to participate in the training institute process, no one should allow his or her "personal preferences" to stand in the way of a system that had shown its potential "to embrace millions of souls from diverse backgrounds."[131]

The message seemed to be addressed at least in part to the United States, where the changes in focus and administrative restructuring over the previous decade had left some believers confused. For example, local communities in a number of areas had instituted relatively elaborate Bahá'í Sunday school programs using the training materials developed at the National Center, and the transition to the more decentralized and outward-looking model assumed by the Ruhi Institute materials often proved to be challenging. In

2007, in order to explain the importance and nature of the training institute process and attempt to build unity of thought around the framework for action, the Universal House of Justice took the highly unusual steps of sending a letter to supersede a portion of the National Spiritual Assembly's annual report and dispatching a member of the International Teaching Center to speak on its behalf to the National Convention and directly to the National Assembly. In the South Carolina community, however, where the imperative of "embrac[ing] millions of souls" remained a strong part of the culture, there had been little of the confusion over methods and materials that affected other parts of the country. In fact, in some respects the state was already ahead: few local communities had an investment in the U.S.-produced materials, the regional training institute had been using the curriculum of the Ruhi Institute's exclusively for several years, and it had been an early adopter of the junior youth program, with groups already up and running in a few localities by the end of the previous plan.[132]

Rather than questions of curriculum, the most significant change in the new Five Year Plan for South Carolina revolved around the status of the Louis G. Gregory Bahá'í Institute. Since the introduction of the new approach to training institutes in 1996, the facility—one of the first institutes established in the world during the Nine Year Plan—had remained in limbo. During the Four Year Plan, the National Spiritual Assembly had decided to reorient the property as a local community center, with programs designed to serve the area around Hemingway. Not surprisingly, participation had declined since then, even with the completion of significant renovations to the campus in the early 2000s. In discussions among the National Spiritual Assembly, the Regional Bahá'í Council, and the Continental Counselors, some raised concerns that the property was no longer useful, was not centrally located, or cost too much to operate. In this context, in the fall of 2005, the National Assembly invited the South Carolina community to advise it on "the future of the Institute." In September, about one hundred people attended a town hall–style meeting with the secretary of the National Assembly and the members of the Regional Council; in addition, dozens of individuals and Local Spiritual Assemblies wrote to the National Assembly to voice their concerns.

"Without exception," the National Assembly reported afterward, "the Bahá'ís of South Carolina expressed a strong desire to see the Institute continue to serve the region and a corresponding will to arise to participate in its programs and serve the process of its development." More than six months of further discussions at the national level, with guidance from the Universal House of Justice, placed the property under the jurisdiction of the Regional Council. The Regional Council, in turn, moved quickly to combine the old and new approaches to training: the familiar name "Louis G. Gregory Bahá'í Institute" would now apply to the whole training institute structure for the Carolinas and Georgia, and the Hemingway campus would serve as its headquarters. The change was beneficial in a number of ways. With access to office, classroom, kitchen, and dormitory space, the training institute staff was able to improve its functioning and expand the schedule of intensive courses and other programs serving the three-state region, while the historic campus gained a new lease on life with a broader geographic scope, an improved administrative structure, and, for the first time in its more than three decades in existence, a proven curriculum. Moreover, the association of the community's new grassroots educational system with both the Hemingway property and its beloved namesake more clearly linked the current approaches to growth with the long history of the faith in South Carolina.[133]

The effects of the change were immediate and dramatic, especially in the Institute's programs for young people. In a letter to the National Spiritual Assembly in October 2005, the Universal House of Justice encouraged the training institutes in the United States to adopt special projects to train youth in the main sequence of courses so that they could "take their rightful place in the forefront of the processes of the Plan, attract their peers to the Cause, and revitalize the community with an influx of young people." Melissa Smith-Venters, the Regional Coordinator for the reorganized Louis Gregory Institute, who was herself a young woman in her early thirties, assembled a small group of collaborators to design such a campaign for the Carolinas and Georgia. Called "Project Mona" after Mona Mahmudnizhad, a sixteen-year-old teacher of Bahá'í children's classes who was executed by the revolutionary regime in Iran in 1983, the first intensive training sessions would focus on increasing the number of youth who could serve as teachers of children's classes and animators of junior youth groups. Beginning in July 2006, Project Mona featured intensive summer sessions lasting more than a week and additional training sessions of various durations during the school year, held at the Hemingway campus and elsewhere.[134]

The elements that characterized Project Mona included the diversity of the participants, with a focus on involving African American youth; reliance on tutors and coordinators who were themselves youth and young adults, which seemed to have a galvanizing effect on the participants; a strong practice component that immediately placed youth in the field of

Project Mona participants with Melissa Smith-Venters, Regional Coordinator of the Louis G. Gregory Bahá'í Institute (*center row, standing, second from left*), and Auxiliary Board member Windi Burgess (*center row, standing, right*), July 2006. *Author's personal collection.*

service in host clusters, for example by teaching an existing children's class or canvassing a neighborhood in order to establish a new one; and integration of the arts across all aspects of the program. Many of the young participants, some of whom were carrying out their first acts of direct service to the faith, reported that this aspect of the training was "their most transforming experience." For other participants, the emphasis on the arts—particularly composing songs based on passages that they were studying from the Bahá'í writings—provided their first meaningful artistic expression of the faith. It was an important moment in the development of a strong Bahá'í identity in a new generation, including many whose parents and grandparents had embraced the faith in the campaigns of the 1970s and 1980s. Moreover, as a result of participation in Project Mona, youth began to take the lead in expansion and consolidation activities in their own clusters—some of which had experienced very little growth in recent years—and a new wave of songs energized the devotional life of local communities across the region.[135]

Perhaps the most dramatic effects of the reorganization of the Louis Gregory Institute were in the Pee Dee cluster—comprising Darlington, Florence, and Williamsburg Counties near the Hemingway campus—an area that had experienced some of the most intensive teaching during the 1970s and 1980s but where Bahá'í community life had ebbed considerably

Musical devotions featuring songs composed during Project Mona at a regional conference in Atlanta, part of a series of forty-one conferences worldwide called by the Universal House of Justice to accelerate progress in the Five Year Plan, 2008. The artistic component of Project Mona energized Bahá'í community life across the region. *Personal collection of Daniel Badi Rinaldi.*

since the 1990s. Efforts to introduce elements of the new framework received a boost in February 2007 when Penelope Walker, a member of the International Teaching Center, visited the area. Some seventy people came to a meeting with her at the Institute campus, during which she called attention to the pivotal place of South Carolina in the country's Bahá'í history. She insisted that a trickle of growth was not commensurate with the area's demonstrated receptivity to the faith and explained the strategy recommended by the International Teaching Center for clusters with a history of large-scale growth: even in localities that had been "dormant for years," teams of teachers could use the membership list as a "starting point" for home visits in order to meet those who were still interested, develop friendships, and establish devotional meetings and study circles, especially with youth. The advice became the Pee Dee cluster's mandate. During 2007 and 2008, more than fifty people in several localities became Bahá'ís, and dozens of others—including many who had embraced the faith years ago but had become inactive—began to participate in a growing range of community activities.[136]

Both Project Mona and the revival of the community in the Pee Dee cluster were part of a national trend that saw an increase in teaching around the country. During 2008 and 2009, several clusters, including in the Atlanta and Phoenix areas, measured their membership growth in the dozens or the hundreds; at the national level, the number of enrollments each year was more than two thousand, approximately the same rate of growth as during Project Tabarsi in the mid-1980s. This time, however, rather than being confined to eastern South Carolina, the new believers were spread much more evenly across the United States, and in addition to large numbers of African Americans, they included many whites, Latinos, and new immigrants. Moreover, the proliferation of the training institute system had given the entire national community as never before a single vocabulary with which to discuss growth and prepared a far larger number of people than there had been in the 1970s to assist with effective consolidation. In November 2010, Bahá'ís from across South Carolina gathered at the College of Charleston to commemorate the centenary of Louis Gregory's first southern teaching trip. With the end of the Five Year Plan just a few months away, it seemed that the growth campaigns of the 1970s and 1980s for which Gregory had presciently laid the groundwork were beginning to bear new fruit, both in his home state and beyond.[137]

THE NEXT HUNDRED YEARS

O ver the long centuries of humanity's collective childhood, it has not been given to every people to witness the rise of a new world religion. Yet the people of South Carolina have been observers of and participants in the emergence of the Bahá'í Faith virtually since its inception in the mid-nineteenth century. Perhaps it is a sort of divine coincidence that their first encounter with a religious movement that calls for the peaceful reconstruction of the whole planet took place when the fires of the War of the Rebellion had barely cooled. To be sure, the abolition of slavery and the extension of citizenship to African Americans during Reconstruction—and the many dramatic improvements in South Carolina's political, economic, educational, and social life that resulted—represented significant and far-reaching steps toward the realization of Bahá'u'lláh's central teaching of the oneness of humanity. But the very successes of black South Carolinians and their progressive white allies in building a new society provoked a violent reaction by upholders of the old order. By the time a child of that same Reconstruction came home to spread the Bahá'í message in earnest in 1910, the Jim Crow regime and the Protestant orthodoxy with which it was intertwined had hardened the state's soil to the new faith.

Over the succeeding decades, as a national Bahá'í community took shape in large part around the imperative of establishing itself in every corner of the country, especially the South, small groups of people in a few of South Carolina's cities and towns—black and white, male and female, northern and southern, native and immigrant, rich and poor—learned to worship, study, teach, and administer their affairs together as equal partners and intimate friends. With limited material resources at their disposal and facing a surprising amount of opposition given their small numbers, South Carolina's Bahá'ís could do little to effect the kind of profound social transformation envisioned in their religion's writings. Yet as they worked to build their own model of grassroots spiritual democracy, they consistently reached out to leaders of thought, proclaimed their message through public lectures and in the mass media, and sought to encourage individuals and organizations in the vanguard of the struggle for civil rights. In the late 1960s, as the worst constraints of the Jim Crow system collapsed, a community with decades' worth of hard-won interracial experience set out to take its message to the masses of the state's population. Thousands of people, most of them African Americans, responded readily to the idea that a new Messenger of God had come with teachings to unite all humanity—part of a worldwide trend in which Bahá'í membership shifted toward Africa, Latin America, and Asia. What ensued was an intensive period of learning for the Bahá'í community, in South Carolina and elsewhere, about how to raise the capacity of a population to take charge of its own spiritual, social, and intellectual development. The fruit of this experimentation was a global system of grassroots education designed to empower growing contingents of people to apply the teachings of the faith to their individual and collective lives. By the centenary of Louis Gregory's fateful trip, the system was beginning to take root in a number of places in South Carolina.

What, then, of the next hundred years of the Bahá'í Faith in South Carolina? Shoghi Effendi's vision of history posits two sets of forces—those of disintegration and of integration—unleashed by the revelations of the Báb and Bahá'u'lláh and at work in the contemporary world. The former tend to sweep away barriers to the realization of the oneness of humanity, often in violent and unpredictable fashion; the latter, often less spectacular but ultimately more important, tend toward the establishment of new patterns of order characterized by unity and justice. These forces, often appearing to operate dialectically, helped to define the world of the twentieth century, and it would be reasonable to expect them to accelerate in the twenty-first. While it is impossible to know with any certainty how new and recurring crises or unimagined opportunities may affect any part of the world even a few years hence, the broad outlines of the framework for action put in place by the Universal House of Justice beginning in the late 1990s are clear enough to be able to speculate about the future of the Bahá'í Faith in South Carolina.[138]

At the time of this writing, the training institute process has begun to engage people in most of the state's geographic clusters. In most areas, however, this involves so far only a few individuals or families—Bahá'ís and their neighbors—participating in the core activities of devotional meetings, children's classes, junior youth groups, and study circles. In a few places, dozens are engaged, and a more dynamic community life is taking shape. What will surely remain the community's primary focus for some time will be initiating a fresh process of growth in the few clusters where it has yet to take root and encouraging its development across the state to involve ever-larger numbers of people in more places. Whether in areas where large-scale growth occurred in decades past or in neighborhoods and towns where the faith has never before had a presence, the process depends on working with people "from every walk of life" who are eager to draw inspiration from the faith's teachings and "dedicate their time and energies to the welfare of humanity," regardless of whether or not they choose to identify themselves as Bahá'ís. In this broader definition of *community* that has emerged more clearly since the 1990s, growth will increasingly be measured not just by a rise in membership but perhaps more meaningfully by the number of those participating in community-building activities. As more people become involved, a natural consequence will be the emergence of a variety of grassroots efforts, according to the needs and interests in each town or neighborhood and in cooperation with others, to participate in the discourses of society and to improve the social, intellectual, and economic life of the population. For example, given the South Carolina Bahá'í community's experience in rural areas beginning in the 1970s and the imperative of reestablishing a strong presence in every geographic cluster, in the coming decades one might expect to see the Bahá'ís contributing to a revitalization of rural life through initiatives in such areas as racial reconciliation, education, housing, sustainable agriculture, the promotion of traditional arts and crafts, and the revival of minority languages such as Gullah and Catawba. Whether undertaken in rural or urban spaces, the type of growth that is envisioned will challenge both the Bahá'ís and their collaborators on the one hand and social scientists and policymakers on the other to conceive of the Bahá'í Faith not only as a discrete religious body with its own beliefs and practices and a recognizable number of adherents but also as a social and cultural movement with ramifications beyond its own membership.[139]

In this context, the establishment and development of Local Spiritual Assemblies, a major focus of successive plans in South Carolina during the 1970s and 1980s, will take on new meaning and relevance. It is reasonable to expect that in many places where a Local Assembly existed in the past, a rising number of participants in the community-building activities engendered by the training institute will recognize the advantages of having such an institution of collective decision making at the local level and will work to reestablish it, this time on a stronger basis than before. In the state's larger towns and cities, growth will likely require the decentralization of such activities as the Nineteen Day Feast and observances of the Holy Days to the level of the neighborhood. When numbers in a single municipality begin to reach into the thousands, the Universal House of Justice has indicated that it may authorize a two-stage election of the Local Spiritual Assembly; one might expect this to eventually be the case in Charleston, Columbia, Florence, Greenville, Spartanburg, and perhaps even some of South Carolina's smaller cities. In large and small localities alike, Bahá'í communities and their elected representatives will surely become more adept at interacting with a range of institutions and agencies—political, cultural, educational, and religious—in their areas and cooperating in endeavors aimed at the common good.[140]

As Local Spiritual Assemblies become more sophisticated in their operations, many of them will need access to modest office facilities, and as activities associated with the training institute multiply in a given neighborhood some dedicated space may become necessary. In general, however, the community's various activities will likely continue to take place in highly decentralized fashion—in homes and in borrowed or rented facilities such as schools, church halls, and community centers rather than through a new network of dedicated Bahá'í Centers. On the other hand, the proliferation of neighborhood devotional meetings may give rise to a new kind of structure on South Carolina's landscape. In 2012, with the construction of the last of the continental Houses of Worship underway in Chile, the Universal House of Justice announced that the gradual establishment of these institutions at the national and local levels would begin around the world. Envisioned in the faith's scriptures as a spiritual center with humanitarian and educational agencies clustered around it, the House of Worship combines "two essential, inseparable aspects of Bahá'í life: worship and service." Over the course of the coming decades, as Bahá'í communities in South Carolina advance in the process of growth and their engagement with the wider society, one might well anticipate that the House of Justice will call for the establishment of a local House of Worship in one or more of the state's clusters.[141]

Experience over the faith's first century in South Carolina indicates that the community has advanced most readily when the administrative agency between the local and the national levels—usually some version of a Regional Teaching Committee, either for South Carolina alone or in combination with its immediate neighboring states—has been robust and effective. The anticipated rise in activity over the coming decades will highlight the need for more statewide coordination. Early establishment of a State Bahá'í Council to serve South Carolina, along with a corresponding revision of the Louis Gregory Institute's area of service, would probably best provide the necessary focus for assuring the sound development of each of the state's clusters; the evolution of Radio Bahá'í to take advantage of a rapidly changing media environment; and, with the increasing involvement of the community in the life of society, the proper representation of the faith in relation to state government, the media, and nongovernmental organizations of various kinds.[142]

ONE PEOPLE

In the preface to his magisterial history of the state, Walter Edgar writes: "I do not believe that there has ever been any intention to create a polity of 'one people' in South Carolina." As evidence, he quite rightly lists the many different groups who have been "excluded from power or marginalized" since the colony's founding in 1670. With this idea in mind, he chooses as the organizing principle for his narrative a somewhat less lofty goal: the attempt, undertaken by many different individuals and groups over the centuries, to establish "the good order and the harmony of the whole community"—even as he acknowledges that such efforts were not always benign and seldom actually included all of South Carolina's people. Edgar's search for a workable frame of analysis for the state's history is understandable, and it is a conundrum shared by historians and laypeople around the world. Certainly, the way one views the past is intimately connected with one's assumptions about human nature and about the direction of humanity's future.[143]

In point of fact, a number of groups—Reconstruction-era lawmakers, communist-inspired labor organizers during the New Deal, and civil rights activists in the mid-twentieth century come readily to mind—aimed to "create a polity of 'one people' in South Carolina." At least since 1910, the state's Bahá'ís, representing an increasingly diverse cross section of its people, have been working to do so consciously, explicitly, and with remarkable consistency along the lines laid out in the sacred scriptures of their faith. That their numbers have usually been quite small and their efforts seldom made the headlines does not mean that they have been any less real. Without any hope for material gain—indeed in many cases, quite the opposite—they have attempted to awaken their friends and neighbors to an appreciation of the fundamental oneness of humanity, with all its implications for the artificial distinctions of race, class, gender, and creed that have so warped South Carolina and the country of which it forms a part. As to "the good order and the harmony of the whole community," South Carolina's Bahá'ís have repeated Bahá'u'lláh's assertion that the "well-being of mankind, its peace and security, are unattainable unless and until its unity is firmly established." In this view, no geographic or demographic portion of South Carolina can hope for true prosperity without addressing the needs of all. In other words, the "whole community" must mean nothing less than the *whole community*; "good order" and "harmony" must not be empty platitudes or worse, rhetorical weapons in the effort of any group to oppress another. More challenging still has been the Bahá'ís' insistence that the principle of oneness necessarily extends not just to the boundaries of the state or even of the country but to those of the planet itself, encompassing every human being and the natural systems upon which our collective life depends. Louis Gregory captured this revolutionary idea—the core principle of the Bahá'í Faith—in an article written during the Great Depression:

> *This Most Great Reconstruction which the majestic Revelation of Bahá'u'lláh brings to view is not black or white or yellow or brown or red, yet all of these. It is the power of divine outpouring and endless perfections for mankind.*[144]

In this sense, the Bahá'ís have indeed been working to make of South Carolinians "one people"—one with each other and one with the whole human race. Given the extraordinary challenges of the twentieth century and beyond, it is an experience that certainly deserves to be acknowledged.[145]

During the century to come, South Carolinians will be faced with numerous existential crises. Some, like the effects of climate change and the limitations of global capitalism, we will share more or less in common with the rest of the world. Others, due in large part to South Carolina's historic role in shaping America's racial caste system, we may have a preponderating role in resolving. Indeed, at the time of this writing, echoes of the Charleston Massacre of 2015 still reverberate throughout a country for which fundamental questions of national identity, of the nature of prosperity, and of our place in the world seem to press themselves on the public consciousness with relentless and increasing urgency. If we are to rise to the challenges of the coming decades, South Carolinians will have to adopt new ways of thinking, new modes of social and political organization, new definitions of who we are, and new conceptions of the common good. In this sense, the purpose of this book has not just been to document the establishment and growth of one relatively obscure religious group among the many in South Carolina but, more importantly, to offer a sketch, tentative at least, of some of the principles and processes that might guide its people's future.

NOTES

Prelude

1. For an account of Columbia in the closing days and immediate aftermath of the Civil War, see Moore, *Columbia and Richland County*, chapters 10 and 11.
2. *Daily Phoenix* (Columbia, SC), June 16, 1865, 1. Special thanks to Steven Kolins for bringing this document to light. For discussion of the original essay and its publication in the United States, see Momen, *Bábí and Bahá'í Religions*, 10.
3. Gregory, "Gift to Race Enlightenment," 36–39.

Introduction

4. The data regarding the Bahá'í Faith as the second-largest religious group in South Carolina are derived from the U.S. Religion Census conducted by the Association of Statisticians of American Religious Bodies (ASARB), http://usreligioncensus.org. For examples of media treatment, see Gustav Niebuhr, "Hemingway Journal: A Little Bit of a Change from Old-Time Religion," *New York Times*, March 31, 2000; Stephanie Harvin, "The Ripple Effect: Influencing the Tide of History," *Charleston (SC) Post and Courier*, February 2, 2003; Paul Bowers, "How a 19th-Century Persian Faith Became the Second-Most Common Religion in Our State," *Charleston*

(SC) City Paper, June 17, 2014; Jennifer Berry Hawes, "How the Bahá'í Faith Became South Carolina's Second-Largest Religion," *Charleston (SC) Post and Courier*, June 21, 2014; Linton Weeks, "The Runner-Up Religions of America," *Protojournalist* blog, National Public Radio website, June 22, 2014; Melissa Rollins, "Bahá'í Faith Is Second Most Prevalent Religion in South Carolina," *Florence (SC) Morning News*, July 19, 2014. Likenesses of Gillespie and McNair appear in the African American Monument on the grounds of the State House, dedicated in 2001, and Audé was awarded the Order of the Palmetto, the state's highest civilian honor, in 2006. Audé withdrew her membership in the Bahá'í Faith in 2010. Moyé, a prominent Black Lives Matter activist, was shot to death in New Orleans in early 2018. For more information on the Louis G. Gregory Bahá'í Museum, see www.louisgregorymuseum.org.

5. For "Carolinian Pentecost," see Stephen W. Angell, review of *No Jim Crow Church: The Origins of South Carolina's Bahá'í Community*, by Louis Venters, *American Historical Review* 121, no. 4 (October 2016): 1301–02.

6. Matthew 16:27; John 10:16; Bahá'u'lláh, *Tablets*, 167.

7. Bahá'u'lláh, *Tablets*, 87. According to the World Religion Database, the Bahá'í Faith was the fastest-growing religion between 1910 and 2010, with an estimated total of more than seven million adherents worldwide in 2010. Bahá'í sources are generally more conservative. (Johnson and Grim, *World's Religions in Figures*, 59).

Chapter 1

8. The authoritative biography of Louis G. Gregory is Morrison, *To Move the World*.

9. *Washington Bee*, November 8, 1905. For Gregory's political activities, see *Washington Bee*, January 1, 1904; April 23, 1904; August 27, 1904; and September 3, 1907.

10. Gregory, "Some Recollections," 1–3.

11. 'Abdu'l-Bahá to Louis Gregory, translated November 17, 1909, Tablets of 'Abdu'l-Bahá, National Bahá'í Archives of the United States, Wilmette, Illinois [hereafter NBA], quoted in Morrison, *To Move the World*, 7. For treatments of 'Abdu'l-Bahá's visit to North America, see Mottahedeh, ed., *'Abdu'l-Bahá's Journey West* and Stockman, *'Abdu'l-Bahá in America*.

12. "News Notes," *Bahai News* 1, no. 18 (February 7, 1911): 9; Sego, "History of the Baha'i Cause," 2.

13. Louis G. Gregory to Joseph A. Hannen, November 9 and 12, 1910, Hannen-Knoblock Family Papers, NBA.

14. Louis G. Gregory to Joseph A. Hannen, November 12, 1910, Hannen-Knoblock Family Papers, NBA; "Attorney Gregory South (From the Charleston Messenger)," *Washington Bee*, November 26, 1910; "He Had Wrong Religion," *Washington Bee*, November 25, 1911; "Afro-American Cullings," *Savannah (GA) Tribune*, February 10, 1912. For a fuller account of Alonzo Twine's life and death, see Venters, *No Jim Crow Church*, 33–41.

15. Alonzo Twine commitment papers, South Carolina State Hospital Commitment Files, South Carolina Department of Archives and History, Columbia.

16. McCandless, *Moonlight, Magnolias, and Madness*, 274–75, 283–84, 287, 294–96; Record of Deaths 1893–1979, South Carolina State Hospital Records, South Carolina Department of Archives and History, Columbia.

17. I.E. Lowery, "Rev. I.E. Lowery's Column," *Southern Indicator* (Columbia, SC), February 19, 1921.

18. Gregory, "Some Recollections," 3; *Washington Bee*, January 7, 1911, and June 24, 1911; "News Notes," *Bahai News* 1, no. 18 (February 7, 1911): 9; Gregory, "Some Recollections," 6. For a treatment of the establishment of the emergence of a Bahá'í national organization, see Stockman, *Bahá'í Faith in America*, vol. 2.

19. Passenger and Crew Lists of Vessels Arriving at New York, New York, 1897–1957, Records of the Immigration and Naturalization Service, National Archives, Washington, D.C.; "Record of the Fourth Annual Convention of Bahai Temple Unity," *Star of the West* 3, no. 5 (June 5, 1912): 5; Daisy Jackson Moore, handwritten note to "George," n.d., Augusta Bahá'í Archives, Augusta, Georgia.

20. Sego, "History of the Baha'i Cause," 2.

21. On the Jackson family and the founding of North Augusta, see McDaniel, *North Augusta*.

22. Sego, "History of the Baha'i Cause," 1; *Augusta (GA) Chronicle*, March 8, 1914.

23. "Tablet for Augusta, Georgia," 'Abdu'l-Bahá to Joseph Hannen, April 18, 1914, Augusta Bahá'í Archives, Augusta, Georgia.

24. Sego, "History of the Baha'i Cause," 1; *Star of the West* 10, no. 18 (February 7, 1920): 331 and 11, no. 11 (September 27, 1920): 174; Sego, "History of the Baha'i Cause," 1; *Augusta (GA) Chronicle*, January 16, 1917; "Seventeenth Annual Convention [1925]," MS, National Convention Files, Office of the Secretary Records, NBA, 63.

25. *Star of the West* 7, no. 10 (September 8, 1916): 85–91. For an account of 'Abdu'l-Bahá and the Bahá'í holy places during World War I, see Maude and Maude, *Servant, General, and Armageddon*.

26. *Star of the West* 7, no. 17 (January 19, 1917): 170 and no. 16 (December 31, 1916): 159, 170; *Charleston (SC) News and Courier*, December 31, 1916; Lau, *Democracy Rising*, 20–26, 34–37; "Catalogue of the Teachers and Pupils of Avery Normal Institute, Charleston, S.C.," June 1899, Avery School Memorabilia Collection, Avery Research Center for African American History and Culture, College of Charleston, South Carolina; Lau, *Democracy Rising*, 47–48; Hemmingway, "Prelude to Change," 221–22.

27. Lau, *Democracy Rising*, 53–58.

28. Louis Gregory to Agnes Parsons, December 16, 1920, Agnes S. Parsons Papers, NBA, quoted in Morrison, *To Move the World*, 137–38; Hudson, *Entangled by White Supremacy*, 133, 142.

29. *Star of the West* 10, no. 6 (June 24, 1919): 100–102.

30. *Star of the West* 10, no. 5 (June 5, 1919): 88–89; *Teaching Bulletin* 1 (November 19, 1919): 1; Evelyn Hardin, "Roy Williams: Teacher in Word and Deed," *South Carolina Regional Bahá'í Bulletin* 5, no. 4 (Summer 1974): 3.

31. Lowery, "Rev. I.E. Lowery's Column," February 19, 1921. Lowery states that the column is a reprint of an editorial in the *Watchman and Defender*. Copies of the *Watchman and Defender* from January and February 1921 have not survived.

Chapter 2

32. Bahá'u'lláh, *Tablets*, 26–27; 'Abdu'l-Bahá, *Will and Testament*, 11.

33. 'Abdu'l-Bahá, *Will and Testament*, 14; Rabbani, *Priceless Pearl*, 55–56, 247–51; *Star of the West* 13, no. 4 (May 17, 1922): 87.

34. Shoghi Effendi, *God Passes By*, 324; Shoghi Effendi, *World Order*, 144. For discussion of the constitutive principles of the Bahá'í administration and its evolution in the United States, see Abizadeh, "Democratic Elections without Campaigns?"; Bramson, "Plans of Unified Action"; and Bramson-Lerche, "Administrative Order."

35. Dahl, "Three Teaching Methods," 4–10.

36. "News of the Cause," *Bahai News Letter* 4 (April 1925): 4; "Seventeenth Annual Convention [1925]," MS, National Convention Files, Office of the Secretary Records, NBA, 61–62.

37. "The Heart of Dixie: Teaching Amity in the South," *Baha'i News* 58 (January 1932): 2–3.

38. "Stanwood Cobb, Eminent Baha'i Lecturer to Speak Here Tuesday," *Augusta (GA) Chronicle*, March 25, 1934; Sego, "History of the Baha'i Cause," 2; Frain, "Baha'i History," 1.

39. Perry, "Robert S. Abbot"; Frain, "Baha'i History," 2.

40. Shoghi Effendi, *Messages to America*, 7–8; *Bahá'í World*, vol. 9, 1940–1944, National Spiritual Assembly, comp., 200–202.

41. Annual Report of the National Teaching Committee, May 1937–April 1938, National Teaching Committee Records, NBA.

42. "Letters from the Guardian," *Bahá'í News* 103 (October 1936): 1; "Public Meetings in Nashville," *Bahá'í News* 105 (February 1937): 2; Albert James, quoted in Morrison, *To Move the World*, 259; "Letters from the Guardian (to the National Spiritual Assembly)," *Bahá'í News* 108 (June 1937): 1–2; Shoghi Effendi, *Advent of Divine Justice*, 33–34.

43. Annual Report of the National Teaching Committee, May 1937–April 1938, National Teaching Committee Records, NBA; Emogene Hoagg to Charlotte Linfoot, March 22, 1940, H. Emogene Hoagg Papers, NBA.

44. Entzminger and Moore interview; National Teaching Committee to Louella Moore, April 17, 1939, private collection of Richard and Doris Morris; "News of the Bahá'í Friends of N.C., S.C., and So. Ga.," December 1941, Columbia Bahá'í Archives, Columbia, South Carolina; Annual Report of the National Spiritual Assembly of the Bahá'ís of the United States and Canada, 1941–1942, Office of the Secretary Records, NBA, 32; *Regional Teaching Bulletin* 9 (April 1, 1943): 2; Annual Report of the National Spiritual Assembly of the Bahá'ís of the United States and Canada, 1942–1943, Office of the Secretary Records, NBA, 28; "The Universal House of Worship," *Palmetto Leader* (Columbia, SC), March 6, 1940; "Traveling Around America," *Palmetto Leader* (Columbia, SC), November 30, 1940; "House of Worship Model Here," *Columbia (SC) Record*, December 20, 1940; "Baha'i Community Observes New Year," *State* (Columbia, SC), March 24, 1942.

45. Christine Bidwell to Alma Knobloch, May 11, 1938, Hannen-Knobloch Family Papers, NBA; Ford interview; Emogene Hoagg to Leroy Ioas, October 4, 1943, H. Emogene Hoagg Papers, NBA; Evelyn Hardin, "Roy Williams: Teacher in Word and Deed," *South Carolina Regional Bahá'í Bulletin* 5, no. 4 (Summer 1974): 3; Assembly Roll, Greenville, S.C., 1943–1944, Local Spiritual Assembly Records, NBA.

46. "Bahá'í Centenary Radio Program," *Bahá'í World*, vol. 10, 1944–1946, comp. National Spiritual Assembly, 175–176; Louella Moore, postcard to Edward Moore, May 24, 1944, author's personal collection; Evelyn Hardin, "Roy Williams: Teacher in Word and Deed" *South Carolina Regional Bahá'í Bulletin* 5, no. 4 (Summer 1974): 3; "Bahai Faith Centennial Is Planned," *Greenville (SC) News*, May 17, 1944.

47. Shoghi Effendi, *Messages to America*, 88; South Carolina State Voting List, 1950, Columbia Bahá'í Archives, Columbia, SC.

48. Entzminger and Montgomery interview; Emogene Hoagg to Leroy Ioas, October 4, 1943, H. Emogene Hoagg Papers, NBA; "Council Talks Sunday Movies," *Greenville (SC) News*, September 26, 1945; Kenneally, "Fifty Years," 14–15; "Greenville, S.C. Group Wins Right to Hold Non-Segregated Meetings," *Bahá'í News* 266 (April 1953): 8.

49. Shoghi Effendi, *Messages, 1950–1957*, 41; Rabbani, ed., *Ministry of the Custodians*, 322, 166. A new wave of persecution in Iran made construction of a House of Worship there impossible. Instead, Shoghi Effendi called for the erection of two new Houses of Worship, one for the African continent in Kampala, Uganda, and one for Australia in Sydney (both completed in 1961). Their counterpart in Frankfurt was completed in 1964.

50. Shoghi Effendi, *Citadel of Faith*, 126–27, 147–48, 154; Shoghi Effendi (through his secretary) to Bahá'í Inter-Racial Teaching Committee, Dorothy Frey, chair, May 27, 1957, Letters of Shoghi Effendi, NBA, quoted in Morrison, *To Move the World*, 294; Shoghi Effendi (through his secretary), *Bahá'í News* 321 (November 1957), insert, quoted in Taylor, ed., *Pupil of the Eye*, 158; Benson interview; Kenneally, "Fifty Years," 9. For *Briggs v. Elliott*, see Kluger, *Simple Justice*, and Hornsby, *Stepping Stone to the Supreme Court*.

51. Etter-Lewis, "Radiant Lights," 55–56; Kenneally, "Fifty Years," 9–12; Abercrombie interview; South Carolina State Voting List, 1963, private collection of Richard and Doris Morris; David R. McLeod to Rex L. Carter, facsimile of letter, *Bahá'í World*, vol. 13, 1954–1963, comp. Universal House of Justice, 692; Certificate of Incorporation of the Spiritual Assembly of the Bahá'ís of Greenville, South Carolina, facsimile of original, *Bahá'í World*, vol. 13, 1954-1963, comp. Universal House of Justice, 654.

52. Young interview; "Bahá'í Directory 1962–1963," *Bahá'í World*, vol. 13, 1954–1963, comp. Universal House of Justice, 1040; South Carolina State Voting List, 1963, private collection of Richard and Doris Morris; Yvonne R. Harrop, personal conversation with author, June 2014; Annual

Report of the National Spiritual Assembly of the Bahá'ís of the United States, 1961–1962, Office of the Secretary Records, NBA, 14; *Area Teaching Committee Bulletin* 4 (June 1963): 2.

53. "Aldermen Hear Opposition to Greenville's 'Pool Zoo,'" *Greenville (SC) Piedmont*, October 17, 1963; "Council Faces Pool Question," *Greenville (SC) News*, July 10, 1964, and related items on July 14, July 15, August 10, and August 12; "Spiritual Singing Convention," *Greenville (SC) News*, September 19, 1964; John Bolt Culbertson to Reverend Martin Luther King Jr., September 11, 1964, King Center online archive, http://www.thekingcenter.org/archive/document/letter-john-bolt-culbertson-mlk.

54. Neumann,"'This Is *"Him"'*"; Thomas interview; Joe Vaughn, "Why I Am a Baha'i, Not a Christian," *Paladin* (Furman University), February 10, 1967, clipping, private collection of Joy F. Benson.

55. King, *Why We Can't Wait*, 128. For scholarly treatments of the "beloved community," see Smith and Zepp, *Search for the Beloved Community*, particularly chapter 6, and Cone, *Martin & Malcolm & America*, especially chapter 8.

Chapter 3

56. Universal House of Justice, *Messages, 1963–1986*, 6.10, 18.1–5.

57. Hollinger, "Bahá'í Communities," xxx; Hampson, "Growth and Spread," 233.

58. Universal House of Justice, *Messages, 1963–1986*, 46.3–4.

59. Jack E. McCants, "Memories of the Deep South Project," MS, author's personal collection; Martin interview; *South Carolina Baha'i Faith State Goals Committtee Newsletter* 3, no. 3 (June–July 1968): 3; Kahn, "Encounter of Two Myths," 244; *South Carolina Baha'i Bulletin*, June 1967, 2; July 1967, 4; October 1967, 1–2; November–December 1967, 1; and January 1968, 4 (all for enrollments); *South Carolina Baha'i Faith State Goals Committee Newsletter* 3, no. 1 (April 1968): 3; no. 2 (June–July 1968): 3; no. 4 (August–September 1968): 3; and no. 5 (November 1968): 2–3 (all for enrollments); Moses Richardson, quoted in Reynolds, *Trudy*, 29.

60. *South Carolina Baha'i Faith State Goals Committee Newsletter* 3, no. 1 (April 1968): 1, 4; *South Carolina Baha'i Faith State Goals Committee Newsletter* 3, no. 4 (August–September 1968): 1–2; *South Carolina Baha'i Faith State Goals Committee Newsletter* 3, no. 5 (November 1968): 1; National Spiritual Assembly of the Bahá'ís of the United States to State Conventions, November 4, 1968, quoted in McMullen, *Bahá'ís of America*, 138.

61. "Southern Teaching Conference," *National Bahá'í Review*, no. 23 (November 1969): 1–4.

62. *American Bahá'í* 1, no. 2 (February 1970): 1, 4; *American Bahá'í* 1, no. 3 (March 1970): 1, 11; *American Bahá'í* 1, no. 4 (April 1970): 1, 4; Reynolds, *Trudy*, 30.

63. Conference flyer, quoted in Reynolds, *Trudy*, 34–35; *American Bahá'í* 1, no. 4 (April 1970): 2; *American Bahá'í* 1, no. 4 (April 1970): 2; *South Carolina State Goals Committee Newsletter* 4, no. 12 (August 1969): 2; *National Bahá'í Review*, no. 30 (June 1970): 3; *American Bahá'í* 1, no. 4 (April 1970): 2.

64. Report of the Southeastern Bahá'í Schools Committee, part of the Annual Report of the National Spiritual Assembly of the Bahá'ís of the United States, 1970–1971, Office of the Secretary Records, NBA, n.p.; *Bahá'í News*, no. 471 (June 1971): 18; Anne Breneman, quoted in Reynolds, *Trudy*, 53; "Religion Preaching Brotherhood Makes Sharp Gains in Dixie," *Baltimore Afro-American*, June 27, 1970; "Bahais Recruit Southern Blacks," *Greenville (SC) News*, June 28, 1970; *American Bahá'í* 1, no. 11 (November 1970): 1, 5, 11; "Three-Month Plan Goals Set for Southern States," *American Bahá'í*, special edition (October 1970): 10–11.

65. Young interview; "Periscope," *American Bahá'í*, February 1971, 13.

66. "Carolina Story," *American Bahá'í*, February 1971, 2–4; Lerone Bennett Jr., "Bahá'í: A Way of Life for Millions," *Ebony* 20, no. 6 (April 1965): 48–56, and booklet of the same name in author's personal collection; Moses Richardson, quoted in Reynolds, *Trudy*, 50; Roger Roff, quoted in Reynolds, *Trudy*, 47–48. The *Ebony* article, originally published under a cover story on the death of Nat King Cole, had already brought the Bahá'í Faith to the attention of African Americans around the United
+ States. The author, Lerone Bennett Jr., was a well-known journalist and author of popular works of African American history. The photographer, Lacey Crawford, and his wife, Ethel, became Bahá'ís as a result of his work on the story, settling in Winnsboro, South Carolina, as pioneers in 1968 and serving subsequently at the Bahá'í World Center. Personal conversation with Ethel Crawford, Columbia, South Carolina.

67. "Carolina Story," *American Bahá'í*, February 1971, 4; Kahn, "Encounter of Two Myths," 252; Chuck Thomas, quoted in Reynolds, *Trudy*, 48; Roger Roff, quoted in Reynolds, *Trudy*, 49; note attributed to Sandy Roff, quoted in Reynolds, *Trudy*, 49.

68. *American Bahá'í*, January 1971, 1; Universal House of Justice, *Messages, 1968–1973*, 65; Annual Report of the National Spiritual Assembly of the Bahá'ís of the United States, 1970–1971, Office of the Secretary

Records, NBA, n.p. On entry by troops, see Shoghi Effendi, *Citadel of Faith*, 107–9, 120.

69. Kahn, "Encounter of Two Myths," 250; *National Bahá'í Review*, no. 40 (April 1971), 2; Annual Report of the National Spiritual Assembly of the Bahá'ís of the United States, 1970–1971, Office of the Secretary Records, NBA, n.p.

70. Roger Roff, quoted in Reynolds, *Trudy*, 51; Kahn, "Encounter of Two Myths," 262–63; Reynolds, *Trudy*, 52; *American Bahá'í*, May 1971, 4–5.

71. Annual Report of the National Spiritual Assembly, *National Bahá'í Review*, no. 53 (May 1972): 1–2; *American Bahá'í*, September 1971, 8; "129: Year of the Final Mighty Thrust—Annual Report of the National Spiritual Assembly [1971–72]," *National Bahá'í Review*, no. 53 (May 1972): 7; *American Bahá'í*, September 1971, 2; *American Bahá'í*, August 1971, 6–7.

72. Young interview; Kahn, "Encounter of Two Myths," 268-73.

73. *American Bahá'í*, January 1972, 5, 10; Universal House of Justice to the National Spiritual Assembly of the Bahá'ís of the United States, February 14, 1972, *National Bahá'í Review*, no. 51 (March 1972): 1, also published in Universal House of Justice, *Messages, 1968–1973*, 85–6.

74. *American Bahá'í*, January 1972, 1, 3; *Bahá'í World*, vol. 14 (1968–1973), 222–23; *National Bahá'í Review*, no. 54 (June 1972): 4; Kahn, "Encounter of Two Myths," 258–60; *American Bahá'í*, April 1971, 8–9.

75. *South Carolina Regional Bahá'í Bulletin*, 'Izzat 129 [September 1972], 4–5, 8.

76. *South Carolina Regional Bahá'í Bulletin*, Qawl 129 [November 1972], 7–9; *South Carolina Regional Bahá'í Bulletin*, 'Izzat 129 [September 1972], 8; Wilbur Vereen, quoted in Reynolds, *Trudy*, 91; *South Carolina Regional Newsletter* 2, no. 5 (December 1972): 1–2; *South Carolina Regional Bahá'í Bulletin*, Qawl 129 [August 1972], 5; *South Carolina Regional Newsletter* 2, no. 4 (November 1972): 1.

77. *South Carolina Regional Bahá'í Bulletin*, 'Izzat 129 [September 1972], 6.

78. *Bahá'í News*, no. 501 (December 1972): 7–8; *American Bahá'í*, November 1972, 2–3; *Bahá'í News*, no. 501 (December 1972): 9.

79. *American Bahá'í*, March 1973, 7; *South Carolina Regional Bahá'í Bulletin* 3, no. 5 (Summer 1973): 2; *South Carolina Regional Bahá'í Bulletin* 3 (April 1973): 1.

80. Hampson, "Growth and Spread," 281; Robert Stockman, "U.S. Bahá'í Community Membership: 1894–1996," *American Bahá'í*, November 23, 1996, 27; *Bahá'í News*, no. 492 (March 1972): 11; "Operation 'Gabriel,'" *American Bahá'í*, January 1972, 3. For a discussion of the increasing diversity of the American Bahá'í community in the 1960s and 1970s, see Hampson, "Growth and Spread," 344–50.

Chapter 4

81. *American Bahá'í*, March 1979, 7. For a sampling of local Bahá'í communities in South Carolina, see *South Carolina Regional Bahá'í Bulletin* 3 (April 1973): 4; 3, no. 6 (Fall/Winter 1974): 7–8; and 5, no. 1 (Spring 1975): 4.

82. Smith, "Bahá'í Faith in the West," 24–26.

83. Universal House of Justice, *Messages 1963–1968*, 124.2; 115.1; 131.1; 132.3; 137.1–6.

84. Universal House of Justice, *Messages, 1963–1986*, 124.2; 137.1-6; 141.4, 11, 13–14.

85. Universal House of Justice to the Bahá'ís of the United States, Naw-Rúz 1974, *National Bahá'í Review*, no. 76 (May 1974): 3–4; National Spiritual Assembly of the Bahá'ís of the United States to the National Teaching Committee, May 17, 1974, *National Bahá'í Review*, no. 82 (November 1974): 2–3; Universal House of Justice to the National Spiritual Assembly of the Bahá'ís of the United States, February 14, 1972, *National Bahá'í Review*, no. 51 (March 1972): 1, also published in Universal House of Justice, *Messages, 1968–1973*, 85–86. The reasons it proved difficult to initiate large-scale growth in places outside the Deep South are unclear; this is an area that calls for further research.

86. McMullen, *Bahá'ís of America*, 156; *South Carolina Regional Bahá'í Bulletin* 4, no. 2 (Summer 1974): 6; Reynolds, *Trudy*, 69, 72.

87. *South Carolina Regional Bahá'í Bulletin* 4, no. 3 (Fall 1974): 3; *South Carolina Regional Bahá'í Bulletin* 5, no. 1 (Fall 1975): 2; *South Carolina Regional Bahá'í Bulletin* 4, no. 1 (Spring 1974): 1.

88. *South Carolina Regional Bahá'í Bulletin* 3, no. 6 (January 1974): 8; Reynolds, *Trudy*, 86.

89. *South Carolina Regional Bahá'í Bulletin* 3 (April 1973): 1; *Regional Newsletter* 1, no. 3 (December 1972): 1; *South Carolina Regional Bahá'í Bulletin* 3, no. 5 (Summer 1973): 4; *South Carolina Regional Bahá'í Bulletin* 4, no. 2 (Summer 1974): 4–5; *South Carolina Regional Bahá'í Bulletin* 5, no. 1 (Fall 1975): 7.

90. *South Carolina Regional Bahá'í Bulletin* 4, no. 1 (spring 1974): 6; *South Carolina Regional Bahá'í Bulletin* 5, no. 1 (spring 1975): 3; *South Carolina Regional Bahá'í Bulletin* 5, no. 3 (Fall 1975): 7; *South Carolina Regional Bahá'í Bulletin* 4, no. 3 (Fall 1974): 2; *Bahá'í News* 52, no. 7 (July 1975): 19; miscellaneous programs and calendars, 1975–1977, author's personal collection.

91. *South Carolina Regional Bahá'í Bulletin* 4, no. 3 (Fall 1974): 2; *South Carolina Regional Bahá'í Bulletin* 3, no. 5 (Summer 1973): 3; *South Carolina Regional*

Bahá'í Bulletin 5, no. 1 (Spring 1975): 3; *South Carolina Regional Bahá'í Bulletin* 5, no. 3 (Fall 1975): 1.

92. *Southern Bahá'í Bulletin*, April 1976, 4.

93. Kahn, "Encounter of Two Myths," 374–76, 386–92; *South Carolina Regional Bahá'í Bulletin* 5, no. 3 (Fall 1975): 4; Reynolds, *Trudy*, 127.

94. *Weekly Observer* (Hemingway, SC), August 28, 1975; Charles Nightingale, quoted in Reynolds, *Trudy*, 78–79; Reynolds, *Trudy*, 108–9.

95. *South Carolina Regional Newsletter* 2, no. 9 [misnumbered] (June 1973): 2; *American Bahá'í*, December 1973, 3–5, 12; *American Bahá'í*, October 1973, 15; *South Carolina Regional Bahá'í Bulletin* 3, no. 6 (January 1974): 4; *South Carolina Regional Bahá'í Bulletin* 3, no. 5 (Summer 1973): 8; *South Carolina Regional Newsletter* 2, no. 9 (October 1973): 1; *American Bahá'í*, December 1973, 12.

96. *South Carolina Regional Bahá'í Bulletin* 4, no. 1 (Spring 1974): 7.

97. *South Carolina Regional Bahá'í Bulletin* 4, no. 2 (Summer 1974): 1, 7; *South Carolina Regional Bahá'í Bulletin* 4, no. 3 (Fall 1974): 6, 8; *South Carolina Regional Bahá'í Bulletin* 5, no. 1 (Spring 1975): 4; Elizabeth Ellis, personal conversation with author, 2016.

98. *South Carolina Regional Bahá'í Bulletin* 5, no. 1 (Spring 1975): 2; *Bahá'í News* 56, no. 8 (August 1975): 20; *South Carolina Regional Bahá'í Bulletin* 5, no. 3 (Fall 1975): 3, 5.

99. *Bahá'í National Review*, no. 99 (April 1976): 1.

100. *Bahá'í News*, no. 539 (February 1976): 11-12; *Bahá'í News*, no. 540 (March 1976): 28-29; *Southern Bahá'í Bulletin*, April 1976, 1. While the number nine holds symbolic meaning in the Bahá'í Faith as the numerical equivalent of the word *bahá*, the choice of states seems to have reflected a perceived need for a strong enough local administrative base to sustain large-scale growth.

101. *Bahá'í News*, no. 542 (May 1976): 17.

102. Kahn, "Encounter of Two Myths," 276, 295–96.

103. Kahn, "Encounter of Two Myths," 315–16, 318, 328–32, 338–40; Bahá'í National Information Office, "Study at Louis G. Gregory Bahá'í Institute, Hemingway, South Carolina, December 26, 1976–January 2, 1977," Office of the Secretary Records, NBA. Exploring the reasons for the failure of Project Outreach will require further research.

104. *American Bahá'í*, September 1977, 4.

105. *American Bahá'í*, March 1978, 6; *American Bahá'í*, March 1979, 7, 9; *Bahá'í News*, no. 575 (February 1979): 11.

106. *American Bahá'í*, March 1983, 10; *American Bahá'í*, September 1983, 1; *American Bahá'í*, January 1984, 8; *American Bahá'í*, February 1984, 1;

American Bahá'í, May 1985, 1; *Bahá'í News*, no. 651 (June 1985): 1-2; South *Carolina Bahá'í, Spring 1986, 2*; Reynolds, *Trudy*, 109; personal conversation with Jerome Glassman.

107. *American Bahá'í*, February 1982, 1; *American Bahá'í*, October 1984, 10; *American Bahá'í*, September 1985, 1; *American Bahá'í*, September 1985, 1.

108. *American Bahá'í*, August 1985, 10; *American Bahá'í*, September 1985, 4.

109. *American Bahá'í*, September 1985, 1, 4. For the development of the Ruhi Institute, see Ruhi Institute, *Learning about Growth.*

110. *American Bahá'í*, August 1985, 10; *American Bahá'í*, December 1983, 25; April 1985, 23. A useful summary of the national community's government-relations efforts on behalf of the Iranian Bahá'ís is McMullen, *Bahá'ís of America*, 169–80. For a sampling of newspaper coverage in South Carolina, see "Baha'i Faith 'Not Sect of Islam,'" *Greenville (SC) News*, January 13, 1979; "Baha'is Voice Concern," *Greenville (SC) News*, May 9, 1981; "Orangeburg Group Assails Iran Regime," *Times and Democrat* (Orangeburg, SC), June 30, 1981; "U.S. Says Baha'i Leaders Executed," *Greenville (SC) News*, December 31, 1981; "The Baha'i Teachings," *Index-Journal* (Greenwood, SC), May 14, 1983; "Baha'is Feel Compassion for Friends, Relatives in Iran," *Greenville (SC) News*, July 2, 1983; "Baha'is Express Concern over Treatment of Iranian Baha'is," *Greenville (SC) News*, June 2, 1984; "Khomeini's Persecution," *Index-Journal* (Greenwood, SC), June 26, 1984.

111. *American Bahá'í*, December 1986, 24; *American Bahá'í*, March 1986, 23; *Bahá'í News*, no. 668 (November 1986): 1.

112. National Spiritual Assembly to the American Bahá'í Community for the Feast of Rahmat, June 24, 1988, quoted in McMullen, *Bahá'ís of America*, 193; McMullen, *Bahá'ís of America*, 197–98.

113. "Louis Gregory Institute, Radio Baha'i Focus on Social Justice, Joy, Happiness," *Florence (SC) Morning News*, September 22, 2017.

114. *American Bahá'í*, Bahá 149 (March–April 1992), 19; *American Bahá'í*, Núr 149 (June–July 1992), 5.

115. *American Bahá'í*, Kalimát 149 (July 1992), 15.

116. Universal House of Justice to the National Spiritual Assembly of the Bahá'ís of the United States, May 19, 1994, http://www.bahai.org/library/authoritative-texts/the-universal-house-of-justice/messages/#d=19940519_001&f=f1.

Chapter 5

117. Universal House of Justice to the Conference of the Continental Boards of Counselors, December 26, 1995, *Turning Point*, 1.3, 1.15.

118. Universal House of Justice to the Bahá'ís of the World, Ridván 1996, *Turning Point*, 4.18.

119. Universal House of Justice to the Conference of the Continental Boards of Counselors, December 26, 1995, *Turning Point*, 1.13–16.

120. "Training Institutes," document prepared for and approved by the Universal House of Justice, April 1998, *Turning Point*, 50.37–45.

121. *Century of Light*, 104; National Spiritual Assembly of the Bahá'ís of the United States to Local Spiritual Assemblies and Registered Bahá'í Groups, July 31, 1996, Louis G. Gregory Bahá'í Institute Archives; Universal House of Justice to National Spiritual Assemblies, May 30, 1997, *Turning Point*, 14.1–37.

122. "Spiritual Institutions: The Unique Nature of Bahá'í Institutions," produced for the National Spiritual Assembly of the Bahá'ís of the United States, 2000, author's personal collection; National Spiritual Assembly of the Bahá'ís of the United States, *United States Bahá'í Directory*, 1996, 1997, 1999, 2001, NBA.

123. *Century of Light*, 109; Universal House of Justice to the Bahá'ís of the World, Ridván 1999, *Turning Point*, 21.2; Universal House of Justice to the Bahá'ís of the World, November 26, 1999, *Turning Point*, 19.5–6.

124. Universal House of Justice to the Bahá'ís of the World, Ridván 2001, *Turning Point*, 25.1; "Gathering in Holy Land Marks Milestone in the Development of the Bahá'í Faith," Bahá'í World News Service, January 16, 2001, http://news.bahai.org/story/131; Universal House of Justice to the Bahá'ís of the World, January 16, 2001, *Turning Point*, 24.4; "With a Dramatic Flourish, Bahá'ís Unveil Majestic Garden Terraces on Mount Carmel," Bahá'í World News Service, May 22, 2001, http://news.bahai.org/story/120; "Faith Notes," *State* (Columbia, SC), May 18, 2001.

125. Universal House of Justice to the Conference of the Continental Boards of Counselors, January 9, 2001, *Turning Point*, 22.1–20.

126. Universal House of Justice to the Conference of the Continental Boards of Counselors, January 9, 2001, *Turning Point*, 22.14–17.

127. Southern Regional Teaching Office, "How Does My 'B' Stage Cluster Advance to the 'A' Stage?"; Auxiliary Board members Barbara V. Sheridan and Shahin Vafai to Local Spiritual Assemblies serving in "A" and "B" clusters in the Carolinas, March 15, 2004; "Greater Columbia Bahá'í

Calendar," Spring 2004; "Bahá'í Community of Greater Columbia Calendar," Fall 2004; Feast of 'Ilm program, Columbia, SC, October 16, 2004 (all in author's personal collection); "Accompaniment in Columbia, South Carolina," parts 1 and 2, video produced by Bahá'í National Center, 2007, www.youtube.com/watch?v=uRwGuKP6wcU and www.youtube.com/watch?v=_7QbkmZvKW4.

128. "Honoring a Pioneer of Racial Harmony," Bahá'í World News Service, February 9, 2003, http://news.bahai.org/story/188.

129. Louis G. Gregory Bahá'í Museum dedication program, February 7–9, 2003, author's personal collection.

130. Universal House of Justice to the Conference of the Continental Boards of Counselors, December 27, 2005, *Turning Point*, 35.1–2.

131. Universal House of Justice to the Conference of the Continental Boards of Counselors, December 27, 2005, *Turning Point*, 35.26; Universal House of Justice to all National Spiritual Assemblies, December 28, 2005, *Turning Point*, 36.2–6.

132. Annual Report of the National Spiritual Assembly of the Bahá'ís of the United States, Ridván 2007; Universal House of Justice to the National Spiritual Assembly of the Bahá'ís of the United States, April 19, 2007, both in author's personal collection. The materials produced at the National Center were called the Core Curriculum. The interventions of the Universal House of Justice in the U.S. Bahá'í community in 2007 and their effects deserve a great deal of further research.

133. National Spiritual Assembly of the Bahá'ís of the United States to the Bahá'ís of South Carolina, August 3, 2005; National Spiritual Assembly of the Bahá'ís of the United States to the Bahá'ís of South Carolina, May 16, 2006, both in author's personal collection.

134. Quoted in Louis G. Gregory Bahá'í Institute, "Project Mona," September 2006, author's personal collection, 1.

135. Louis G. Gregory Bahá'í Institute, "Project Mona," September 2006, author's personal collection, 2–3; *Southern Breeze* 5, no. 3 (November 2006): 6; Greenville/Spartanburg Priority Cluster Growth Profile, January 2008, author's personal collection.

136. Pee Dee cluster reflection gathering agenda, January 7, 2007, author's personal collection; International Teaching Center, "Building Momentum: A Coherent Approach to Growth," *Turning Point*, 52.36–41; Pee Dee Priority Cluster Growth Profiles, July 2007, October 2007 and January 2008, author's personal collection.

137. Annual Report of the National Spiritual Assembly of the Bahá'ís of the United States, Ridván 2009, author's personal collection; South Carolina Bahá'í Centennial Celebration program, November 13, 2010, author's personal collection.

Afterword

138. See the essays collected in Shoghi Effendi, *World Order of Bahá'u'lláh.*
139. Universal House of Justice to the Bahá'ís of the World, Ridván 2008, http://universalhouseofjustice.bahai.org/ridvan-messages/20080421_001.
140. Universal House of Justice to the Conference of the Continental Boards of Counselors, December 27, 2005, *Turning Point*, 35.20.
141. "Plans to Build New Houses of Worship Announced," Bahá'í World News Service, April 22, 2012, http://news.bahai.org/story/906.
142. South Carolina has been served by the Regional Bahá'í Council of the Southern States and, after splitting the region in two in 2008, the Regional Bahá'í Council of the Southeastern States. Further subdivision of the Southeast in 2012 (Atlantic States) and 2016 (Appalachian States) did not affect South Carolina.
143. Edgar, *South Carolina*, xx. The phrase is borrowed from the legislation that founded South Carolina College (the future University of South Carolina) in 1801, ironically, a project designed to consolidate the power of the plantation aristocracy. For a recent treatment of the origins and purpose of South Carolina College, see Dorn, *For the Common Good*, chapter 2.
144. Gregory, "Gift to Race Enlightenment," 39.
145. Bahá'u'lláh, *Gleanings*, 346; Edgar, *South Carolina*, xx.

BIBLIOGRAPHY

Primary Sources

'Abdu'l-Bahá. *The Will and Testament of 'Abdu'l-Bahá*. Wilmette, IL: Bahá'í Publishing Trust, 1990.

Abercrombie, J. Richard. Interview by author, December 7, 2003, Greenville, South Carolina.

Bahá'u'lláh. *Gleanings from the Writings of Bahá'u'lláh*. 1ˢᵗ pocket-sized ed. Wilmette, IL: Bahá'í Publishing Trust, 1990.

———. *Tablets of Bahá'u'lláh Revealed after the Kitáb-i-Aqdas*. Translated by Habib Taherzadeh. 1ˢᵗ pocket-sized ed. Wilmette, IL: Bahá'í Publishing Trust, 1988.

"Catalogue of the Teachers and Pupils of Avery Normal Institute, Charleston, S.C.," June 1899, Avery School Memorabilia Collection, Avery Research Center for African American History and Culture, College of Charleston, South Carolina.

Entzminger, Jessie Dixon, and Louise Moore Montgomery. Interview by Doris Morris, n.d. [circa 1980s], Columbia, South Carolina. Audio cassette, Columbia Bahá'í Archives, Columbia, South Carolina.

Ford, Virginia. Interview by Elmer Kenneally, 1989, Greenville, South Carolina. Audio cassette, Greenville Bahá'í Archives, Greenville, South Carolina, and notes by Frances Worthington, author's personal collection.

Frain, Marie. "Baha'i History of Augusta, Georgia." MS, Augusta Bahá'í Archives, Augusta, Georgia.

Gregory, Louis G. "A Gift to Race Enlightenment." *World Order* 2, no. 1 (April 1936): 36–39.

———. "Some Recollections of the Early Days of the Bahai Faith in Washington, D.C.," MS, Louis G. Gregory Papers, National Bahá'í Archives of the United States, Wilmette, Illinois.

Hannen-Knoblock Family Papers. National Bahá'í Archives of the United States, Wilmette, Illinois.

Hoagg, H. Emogene. Papers. National Bahá'í Archives of the United States, Wilmette, Illinois.

Kenneally, Elmer. "Fifty Years of the Bahá'í Faith in Greenville, SC, 1939–1989." MS, Greenville Bahá'í Archives, Greenville, South Carolina.

King, Martin Luther, Jr. *Why We Can't Wait*. New York: Harper & Row, 1963.

Local Spiritual Assembly Records. National Bahá'í Archives of the United States, Wilmette, Illinois.

Martin, Elizabeth. Interview by author, April 5, 2003, Columbia, South Carolina.

McCants, Jack E. "Memories of the Deep South Project." MS, author's personal collection.

National Spiritual Assembly of the Bahá'ís of the United States and Canada, comp. *The Bahá'í World: A Biennial International Record*. Vol. 9, *1940–1944*. Wilmette, IL: Bahá'í Publishing Trust, 1981. First published 1945.

———. *The Bahá'í World: A Biennial International Record*. Vol. 10, *1944–1946*. Wilmette, IL: Bahá'í Publishing Trust, 1981. First published 1949.

National Teaching Committee Records. National Bahá'í Archives of the United States, Wilmette, Illinois.

Office of the Secretary Records. National Bahá'í Archives of the United States, Wilmette, Illinois.

Passenger and Crew Lists of Vessels Arriving at New York, New York, 1897–1957. Records of the Immigration and Naturalization Service, National Archives, Washington, D.C.

Rabbani, Rúhíyyih, ed. *The Ministry of the Custodians, 1957–1963: An Account of the Stewardship of the Hands of the Cause*. Haifa, Israel: Bahá'í World Center, 1992.

Sego, Esther. "History of the Baha'i Cause in Augusta, Ga." MS, Augusta Bahá'í Archives, Augusta, Georgia.

Shoghi Effendi. *The Advent of Divine Justice*. 1st pocket-sized ed. Wilmette, IL: Bahá'í Publishing Trust, 1990.

———. *Citadel of Faith: Messages to America, 1947–1957*. Wilmette, IL: Bahá'í Publishing Trust, 1997.

———. *God Passes By*. Wilmette, IL: Bahá'í Publishing Trust, 1974.

———. *Messages to America: Selected Letters and Cablegrams Addressed to the Bahá'ís of North America, 1932–1946.* Wilmette, IL: Bahá'í Publishing Committee, 1947.

———. *Messages to the Bahá'í World, 1950–1957.* Wilmette, IL: Bahá'í Publishing Trust, 1971.

———. *The World Order of Bahá'u'lláh: Selected Letters.* 1ˢᵗ pocket-sized ed. Wilmette, IL: Bahá'í Publishing Trust, 1991.

South Carolina State Hospital Commitment Files. South Carolina Department of Archives and History, Columbia, South Carolina.

South Carolina State Hospital Records. South Carolina Department of Archives and History, Columbia, South Carolina.

Taylor, Bonnie J., ed. *The Pupil of the Eye: African Americans in the World Order of Bahá'u'lláh.* Riviera Beach, FL: Palabra Publications, 1998.

Thomas, June Manning. Interview, May 2014. Commemorating Desegregation at Furman. http://www.furman.edu/about/commemorating-desegregation-at-furman/Pages/June-Manning-Thomas.aspx.

Universal House of Justice. *Messages from the Universal House of Justice, 1963–1986: The Third Epoch of the Formative Age.* Compiled by Geoffry Marks. Wilmette, IL: Bahá'í Publishing Trust, 1996.

———. *Messages from the Universal House of Justice, 1968–1973.* Wilmette, IL: Bahá'í Publishing Trust, 1976.

———. *Turning Point: Selected Messages of the Universal House of Justice and Supplementary Material, 1996–2006.* West Palm Beach, FL: Palabra Publications, 2006.

Universal House of Justice, comp. *The Bahá'í World: An International Record.* Vol. 13, *1954–1963.* Haifa, Israel: Universal House of Justice, 1970.

Young, Jordan, and Annette Young. Interview by author, September 25, 2003, Easley, South Carolina.

Secondary Sources

Abizadeh, "Democratic Elections without Campaigns? Normative Foundations of National Bahá'í Elections." *World Order* 37, no. 1 (2005): 7–49.

Bramson, Loni. "The Plans of Unified Action: A Survey." In *Bahá'ís in the West,* edited by Peter Smith, 154–97. Los Angeles: Kalimát Press, 2004.

Bramson-Lerche, Loni. "Some Aspects of the Development of the *Bahá'í* Administrative Order in America, 1922–1936." In *Studies in Bábí and Bahá'í History.* Vol. 1, edited by Moojan Momen, 254–300. Los Angeles: Kalimát Press, 1982.

Century of Light. Commissioned by the Universal House of Justice. Wilmette, IL: Bahá'í Publishing Trust, 2000.

Cone, James H. *Martin & Malcolm & America: A Dream or a Nightmare*. Maryknoll, NY: Orbis Books, 1991.

Dahl, Roger. "Three Teaching Methods Used during North America's First Seen Year Plan." *Journal of Bahá'í Studies* 5, no. 3 (1993): 1–16.

Dorn, Charles. *For the Common Good: A New History of Higher Education in America*. Ithaca, NY: Cornell University Press, 2017.

Edgar, Walter. *South Carolina: A History*. Columbia: University of South Carolina Press, 1998.

Etter-Lewis, Gwendolyn. "Radiant Lights: African-American Women and the Advancement of the Bahá'í Faith in the U.S." In *Lights of the Spirit: Historical Portraits of Black Bahá'ís in North America, 1898–2000*, edited by Gwendolyn Etter-Lewis and Richard Thomas. Wilmette, IL: Bahá'í Publishing, 2006.

Hampson, Arthur. "Growth and Spread of the Bahá'í Faith." PhD diss., University of Hawaii, 1980.

Hemmingway, Theodore. "Prelude to Change: Black Carolinians in the War Years, 1914–1920." *Journal of Negro History* 65, no. 3 (Summer 1980): 212–27.

Hollinger, Richard. "Introduction: Bahá'í Communities in the West, 1897–1992." In *Community Histories*, edited by Richard Hollinger, vii–xlix. Los Angeles: Kalimát Press, 1992.

Hornsby, Benjamin F. *Stepping Stone to the Supreme Court: Clarendon County, South Carolina*. Columbia: South Carolina Department of Archives and History, 1992.

Hudson, Janet. *Entangled by White Supremacy: Reform in World War I–Era South Carolina*. Lexington: University Press of Kentucky, 2009.

Johnson, Todd, and Brian J. Grim. *The World's Religions in Figures: An Introduction to International Religious Demography*. West Sussex, UK: Wiley-Blackwell, 2013.

Kahn, Sandra Santolucito. "Encounter of Two Myths: Baha'i and Christian in the Rural American South—A Study in Transmythicization." PhD diss., University of California, Santa Barbara, 1977.

Kluger, Richard. *Simple Justice*. New York: Random House, 1977.

Lau, Peter F. *Democracy Rising: South Carolina and the Fight for Black Equality since 1865*. Lexington: University Press of Kentucky, 2006.

Maude, Roderick, and Derwent Maude. *The Servant, the General, and Armageddon*. Oxford: George Ronald, 1998.

McCandless, Peter. *Moonlight, Magnolias, and Madness: Insanity in South Carolina from the Colonial Period to the Progressive Era*. Chapel Hill: University of North Carolina Press, 1996.

McDaniel, Jeanne M. *North Augusta: James U. Jackson's Dream*. Charleston, SC: Arcadia Publishing, 2006.

McMullen, Mike. *The Bahá'ís of America: The Growth of a Religious Movement*. New York: New York University Press, 2015.

Momen, Moojan. *The Bábí and Bahá'í Religions, 1844–1944: Some Contemporary Western Accounts*. Oxford: George Ronald, 1981.

Moore, John Hammond. *Columbia and Richland County: A South Carolina Community, 1740–1990*. Columbia: University of South Carolina Press, 1992.

Morrison, Gayle. *To Move the World: Louis G. Gregory and the Advancement of Racial Unity in America*, Wilmette, IL: Bahá'í Publishing Trust, 1982.

Mottahedeh, Negar, ed. *'Abdu'l-Bahá's Journey West: The Course of Human Solidarity*. New York: Palgrave Macmillan, 2013.

Neumann, Brian. "'This Is "*Him*:'" The Life of Joseph Allen Vaughn." Commemorating Desegregation at Furman. http://www2.furman.edu/about/commemorating-desegregation-at-furman/Road-to-Desegregation/Documents/ThisisHim.pdf.

Perry, Mark. "Robert S. Abbot and the Chicago Defender: A Door to the Masses." *Michigan Chronicle*, October 10, 1995. http://bahai.uga.edu/News/101095.html.

Rabbani, Rúhíyyih. *The Priceless Pearl*. 2nd ed. Oakham, UK: Bahá'í Publishing, 2000.

Reynolds, Annette. *Trudy and the Bahá'ís' Spiritual Path in South Carolina*. Bloomington, IN: Xlibris, 2015.

Ruhi Institute. *Learning about Growth: The Story of the Ruhi Institute and Large-Scale Expansion of the Bahá'í Faith in Colombia*. Riviera Beach, FL: Palabra Publications, 1991.

Smith, Kenneth L., and Ira G. Zepp Jr. *Search for the Beloved Community: The Thinking of Martin Luther King, Jr.* Lanham, MD: University Press of America, 1986.

Smith, Peter. "The Bahá'í Faith in the West: A Survey." In *Bahá'ís in the West, Studies in the Bábí and Bahá'í Religions*, vol. 14, ed. Peter Smith, 3–60. Los Angeles: Kalimát Press, 2004.

Stockman, Robert H. *'Abdu'l-Bahá in America*. Wilmette, IL: Bahá'í Publishing, 2012.

———. *The Bahá'í Faith in America*. Vol. 2, *Early Expansion, 1900–1912*. Oxford: George Ronald, 1995.

Venters, Louis. *No Jim Crow Church: The Origins of South Carolina's Bahá'í Community*. Gainesville: University Press of Florida, 2015.

INDEX

junior youth groups 139
origins and scope 127–131, 132
Ruhi Institute 117, 129, *136*, 139–141
study circles 129, 136
Tucker, William 59
Tuskegee, AL 46
Twelve Month Plan (2000-2001) 131, 132
Twine, Alonzo Edgar 27–30, *28*, *29*, 38, 109

U

Union, SC 107
Universal House of Justice 40, *41*, 63, 79, 90–91, 101, 118, 120–121, 128, 130, 148
and Auxiliary Board members 91, 96
and Continental Board of Counselors 84
and National Spiritual Assembly of U.S. 80, 124, 141–142
and Regional Bahá'í Councils 129
on children and youth 91, 139, 142
on Five Year Plan (1974–1979) 90–92, 111
on geographic clusters 132
on growth in SC 75, 80
on Houses of Worship 150
on Local Spiritual Assemblies 91, 130, 150
on new series of global plans 90, 125, 127, 128, 131, 132, 139
on Nine Year Plan 63–66, 82, 128

on social and economic development 115
on training institutes 128, 140, 141, 142
origins 20, 40, 54
Promise of World Peace 119, 121
University of South Carolina 11, 44, 106
Urban League 36
urban uprisings 65, 67, 122

V

Van Wyck, SC 83
Vaughn, Joseph *60*, 61
Vereen, Ilena 83
Vereen, Wilbur 83
von der Heidt, Grace *52*

W

Wade Hampton Hotel, Columbia, SC 105
Walker, Penelope 144
Washington, D.C. 21, 22–23, 25, 27, 31–32, 34, 37, 44, 46
and Reconstruction 22
race and Baha'i community in 25, 30, 32, 36, 46
Watson, Bransford 98
Watson, Thomas E. 33
Waverly neighborhood, Columbia, SC 48, *49*
Wesson, Vivian 99
Westendorff, Clarence W. *43*, 43–44, 48
Wheeler, Alta 48, *49*

Y

About the Author

L ouis Venters, PhD, teaches African and African diaspora history, southern U.S. history, and public history at Francis Marion University and is a consultant in the fields of historic preservation and cultural resource management. He is the author of *No Jim Crow Church: The Origins of South Carolina's Bahá'í Community* (2015) and the author or coauthor of several site studies, public history reports, and exhibits, including the multiple-award-winning greenbookofsc.com. He is a member of the South Carolina African American Heritage Commission and of the board of directors of Preservation South Carolina. He first encountered the Bahá'í Faith as a young teenager, and since then, he has served in a number of elected and appointed positions in the Bahá'í community and lived and traveled widely in Africa, the Americas, and Europe. He blogs on issues related to race, religion, history, and culture at louisventers.com.

Visit us at
www.historypress.com